DEFEND YOURSELF!

DEFEND YOURSELF!

Every Woman's Guide to Safeguarding Her Life

MATT THOMAS, DENISE LOVEDAY & LARRY STRAUSS

Photographs by Mario Prado

AVON BOOKS ▲ NEW YORK

DEFEND YOURSELF is an original publication of Avon Books. This work has never before appeared in book form.

AVON BOOKS
A division of
The Hearst Corporation
1350 Avenue of the Americas
New York, New York 10019

Copyright © 1995 by Matt Thomas, Larry Strauss, and Denise Loveday
Interior photographs by Mario Prado
Published by arrangement with the authors
Library of Congress Catalog Card Number: 94-34818
ISBN: 0-380-77458-5

Library of Congress Cataloging in Publication Data:

Thomas, Matt.
  Defend yourself / by Matt Thomas, Larry Strauss, and Denise Loveday.
     p.   cm.
1. Self-defense for women.   I. Strauss, Larry.   II. Loveday, Denise.   III. Title.
GV1111.5.T46   1995   94-34818
613.6'6—dc20   CIP

First Avon Books Trade Printing: March 1995

Contents

Foreword

I HAVEN'T BEEN in a fight or serious encounter since the second grade. (I lost that fight because I simply didn't know how to respond.) Since then, I've studied a variety of martial arts, sampling and appreciating each tradition. I've learned enough to recognize brilliance when I see it, and I see its many facets in the authors of this book. Matt Thomas, who shares a lifetime of experience, is a genuine article, and so is this work.

Many experienced martial artists, even masters of their schools, have written books on the philosophy and practice of a particular art, offering self-defense guidance. Each offers the benefit of his individual experience. But I don't know of anyone, anywhere, whose background, intelligence, and heart can better convey the powerful principles and skills than Matt Thomas's. I believe *Defend Yourself* is destined to become a classic in its field.

In order to appreciate, and allow yourself to make use of, this book, you may have to balance conflicting beliefs, values, and philosophies, such as nonviolent ideals versus reality of the streets. In an ideal world, people would be kind and reasonable, threatening you only if provoked. In an ideal world, you could avoid trouble and ensure your own safety simply by being friendly and peaceful.

But the fact is that sometimes trouble finds us. Maybe it happens once in a lifetime, maybe never. For some people, clinging to nonviolent philosophies and keeping their fingers crossed works. But predators do exist in this world, and their numbers are growing. They will attack you because you are a woman, because they are on drugs, need money, had a lousy childhood— or simply because they think they can. And at a time like that, idealism turns to realism pretty fast.

You probably won't be threatened this week, or next, or maybe ever. But it's better to be prepared for a situation that never arises than to be unprepared if it does.

I believe that self-defense is a basic life skill, a form of preventative medicine, like learning how to brush your teeth or take vitamins. In that sense, this book may be the best life insurance policy you've ever purchased.

Two very different attitudes may cause someone to set this book aside; let's examine both. The first can state, "I know this already. I've had self-defense training/I take karate/I've read three books on the subject." The second says, "Anyone knows that if some huge guy attacks you, especially if he's armed, no book is going to do you any good unless you hit him with it."

The authors clearly address these opposing, and potentially paralyzing, beliefs. They are authorities in the truest sense—they speak from in-depth experience, not just hopeful philosophy. I've taken the Model Mugging courses; I know what they have to offer are treasures of practical wisdom that really work.

If you believe that delving into the realities of survival and defense will somehow "attract" violence, then take another look. Some of the most dedicated self-defense students became dedicated after they were mugged or raped. There's no reason to wait for that kind of wake-up call.

The decision to take your life in your hands requires a period of time and commitment; it requires more than a little courage. But once you learn the basic techniques in this book, you become a different kind of person—more balanced, powerful, and self-assured. That confidence can translate into other areas of life. You learn to respect your boundaries and to stand up for yourself in verbal encounters. Best of all, you learn how to avoid trouble in the first place.

The impulse to defend yourself comes from the understanding that *no one has the right to hurt you.* Not if they are bigger than you, not if they had a tough childhood, not if they are rich or famous, not even if they are married to you. No one has that right.

But there are people who may try to hurt you anyway, or hurt someone you care about. Whether the act is right or wrong, passionate or premeditated, justified or insane, they may do so simply because they have the physical power to do so and think of you as defenseless.

As the authors clearly state, you are never defenseless; you have powerful survival instincts. This book doesn't give you anything you don't already have, but it shows how to unleash and channel your instincts in ways that really work.

It's time to take back your power, because *you have a right and a duty to protect yourself and those you love.* The only thing you are guaranteed to keep your entire lifetime is your body. It seems wise to take care of it.

Self-defense means more than avoiding or fending off an attacker. It also means taking care of the body through a healthful diet, regular exercise, rest, and relaxation. In fact, we may have to defend ourselves from a verbal or physical assault only on rare occasions, but we need to defend ourselves from stress every day. The authors understand all this, and present the bigger picture of self-defense. Their techniques can make a very real difference in your life.

This book is written from the heart as well as from the mind, out of a sense of compassion and service. Matt Thomas comes from the best of the peaceful-warrior lineage, dedicated to protecting life, not taking it. Let it be your wake-up call. Let it train and inspire you to new heights of awareness and personal power. You'll be far less likely than ever before to encounter violence and its aftermath.

I consider myself a pacifist, committed to nonviolent solutions to problems or differences. But it seems to me that true pacifists are those who know how to defend themselves, and who can make an informed, courageous *choice* to inflict little or no injury on another. Those who bury their heads in the sand of a nonviolent philosophy may find their beliefs tested harshly in the cold light of day.

It's easy to surround ourselves with hedges and buffers. We may live in a nice neighborhood where violence happens only to other people. But life can be intense, and you just never know.

The empowerment of women this book supports empowers us all to open up to a world of love and mutual respect rather than one of fear and suspicion.

This book is for all those who seek a higher level of confidence, courage, and compassion so they, too, can live like peaceful warriors, secure in the knowledge that they can, if called upon, protect themselves and their loved ones.

Dan Millman
Fall, 1994

DEFEND YOURSELF!

INTRODUCTION

Reaching Within

CAN SELF-DEFENSE BE learned from a book?

To answer that question, we have to look at how people can develop the ability to protect themselves from physical harm. It begins with a person's own survival instinct. Every human—and, for that matter, every animal—has a powerful drive to survive.

When my first child was four days old, I watched him suckling at his mother's breast. It filled my heart with wonder and joy and I tenderly touched my cheek to his. He figured I was going for his milk supply, so he pushed my nose away with the heel of his palm. I was surprised. I tried to cuddle again and he did it again. When I tried it a third time, his mother whacked me on the head, because she said every time I tried that, he clamped down hard! Yes, all of us were born with the instinct to survive, and our parents possessed instincts to keep us alive!

If you are alive today, it is, in part, because hundreds of generations of your ancestors fought and killed out of self-preservation. Self-defense *can* be learned from a book because it comes from within you. This book can guide your discovery of what your mind and body already know.

Even if you only read this book and don't attempt or practice any of the moves, some tip might help you someday. One woman heard me speak briefly on the radio. Two weeks later she was attacked, so she took my advice to drop to the ground and kick. Her assailants fled.

1

If you do the exercises by yourself, there is a greater probability that your body will actually learn muscle reflexes that could save your life.

However, the best way to learn from this book is to first discuss the mental and emotional exercises with a close friend. Next, do the physical exercises in extremely slow motion with your friend, taking turns being the attacker and the defender. It's amazing how, by practicing the correct technique in slow motion, you can speed up the same motions in an emergency.

During the past twenty-four years, more than six thousand women have studied self-defense with me, and over twenty thousand women have studied with former students of mine. My own martial arts training goes back thirty-two years, during which time I have obtained black belts in four fighting styles and studied twenty-two other systems. But the self-defense system herein was not founded on a mat in a martial arts studio. It was founded in an orphanage in Japan.

I was born in occupied Japan, to a Japanese mother and a Russian father serving in the American armed forces, just after the end of World War II. When I was two, my father abandoned us. My mother tried to care for me, but it was extremely difficult. She was shunned by her family and neighbors for bearing the child of a white man. By the time I was three, she found it impossible to provide me with food and shelter and was forced to make the painful decision of placing me in an orphanage. Being among the youngest, I was easy prey for the older boys. They stole food from me during the day and sexually abused me at night. At first I was helpless to defend myself and would just shut down, try to pretend it wasn't happening to me. Soon my survival instincts emerged and I found ways to fend off the older boys. I bit. I kicked. I used improvised weapons, like sticks and rocks. I made simple rope traps to warn me of their approach. I tried to make the act of abusing me almost as unpleasant for my attackers as it was for me—and after a while they left me alone. That was, perhaps, the most profound discovery I would ever make about self-defense. No matter how small I was, or how large and strong my attackers, I had weapons I could use. I was not helpless, and neither is any woman.

My next lesson about self-defense came through the women who ran the orphanage. They were called "the watchers," and though they had probably never read *Oliver Twist* or *Nicholas Nickleby*, they ran that place in true Dickensian style. They fed and clothed us poorly, took in money from two governments and others, and managed to pocket most of it. In order to keep us in line and keep our mouths shut, they beat us regularly, would almost drown us in the hot tubs, and used other oppressive fear tactics. They told us about demons—called *oni*—who would eat us if we didn't behave ourselves. Then, at night, we would be attacked by scary-looking creatures in black robes, with green faces, red eyes, horns, and fangs. They would dance and shriek and lunge at us as we cried and screamed in our beds—and the watchers would fight them off for us.

I was terrified of those demons. What if the watchers didn't come to protect me one night? My fear was so great that I would wet my bed—until the discomfort got to me and I started urinating on the floor instead. One night I urinated on one of the *oni*. It recoiled and screamed like a woman. It grabbed me, so I bit. The *oni* dropped me. My cribmate, Carlos, and I were then wrapped in blankets and shaken. We thought we were being eaten alive. I passed out, and the next day was told that I was so bad the *oni* had spit me out, but that Carlos had been eaten. I started to cry, then heard crying from the next room. It was Carlos! They had told him the same story. We got together and decided to run away. We sneaked into the watchers' closet to steal food and clothes, but the *oni* were right there, waiting for us. We started to scream, then realized that they weren't real. They were only masks and capes. And so my second lesson about self-defense was to know and understand the enemy—to remove his or her power by getting beneath the facade.

I was eventually adopted by an American family and moved to the United States, the land of searchers and dreamers and, of course, amazing grocery stores. Since we were a military family, we moved constantly. I faced many challenges as an immigrant and "half-breed." In Japan, being half European had made me a target; here, being half Japanese had the same effect. I could easily defeat the American bullies; they weren't used to "Orphanage-Fu." But I still felt "less-than" until an English teacher told me that instead of fighting others, I could prove myself through my hard work at school and in athletics. It worked! I was also able to channel a lot of my anger and frustration when I began to study the martial arts in my early teens. By the age of sixteen, I had become a black belt in judo—and an amazing thing happened: nobody picked on me anymore. As soon as I was able to do serious damage to an attacker, somehow the bullies—the cowards—seemed to know, and they avoided me. This was the third very important self-defense lesson life taught me. The best defense is avoidance, and the ability to avoid trouble goes hand in hand with being ready to handle it if and when.

This knowledge and my love of the martial arts brought me to my fourth lesson—the one that directly inspired the inception of my (role) Model Mugging self-defense program for women. It happened when I was twenty-one years old. I was a student at Stanford University and still studying the martial arts. During summer vacation I was training in southern California. One night, a female black-belt student entered the dojo in the middle of the black-belt circle. She was visibly upset. She said that she had been raped and that despite her fighting skills, she had been unable to defend herself against the attacker. This stunned me and all the other students. Here was this black belt whom we had all seen perform beautifully in the dojo, yet who was totally powerless at the moment when she needed her power. Everyone was silent, waiting to see what the master would say, how he would explain why one of his best students was so unprepared for a real-life battle. But the master did not explain. Instead, he agreed with her that her "failure" had shamed us all and that she needed to train harder. She ran away crying, and I went after her, to try to offer some kind of support. The master called out my name as I reached the door. I turned around, and his eyes told me that if I left, I should not return.

I left. And though there was little I could do for the rape victim—in fact, she became angry with me, called me stupid for making the situation worse—I did not regret my actions. I began to question the effectiveness of the martial arts currently being taught as a competitive sport instead of as a defense against rapists and other real-life attackers of our day and age. If all the training this woman had undergone could not make a difference on the streets, then could any woman believe that martial arts were preparing her for battle? Was this woman an anomaly? It got me wondering. Many women do study the martial arts specifically for the purpose of defending themselves against a rapist or other attacker. Yet about 90 percent of what the martial arts teach assumes a vertical position. We stand, we bow, then we fight. Considering this, what occurred to me was, how many women are raped standing up?

Having access to the Stanford University libraries and computer data bases, I spent the next months doing extensive research on attacks against women. I analyzed more than three thousand assaults against women—and confirmed my suspicions. In 40 percent of all such attacks, the victim was knocked to the ground before she knew what had happened. Furthermore, over 80 percent of the attackers used only verbal intimidation, including vulgarity, to scare the victim into submission—something karate, judo, and kung fu do not prepare one for. This was the tip of the iceberg. In my research, I also discovered that some women, despite having no formal self-defense training, were able to defend themselves against an attacker.

This at first seemed surprising. But then, looking at it in a historical context, I found it made sense. The martial arts themselves did not just happen. Each fighting style was developed by a specific group of people, usually oppressed, out of a specific need to defend themselves with their bare hands against an armed oppressor.

- Kung fu was developed by priests, who were vulnerable because they were forbidden to carry edged weapons by their local warlords. It was called sword control and was intended to stop crime and political rebellion. Bandits, who didn't give a darn about sword-control laws and cared even less about the laws against attacking priests, would frequently rob the priests of the alms to build their temples—until the priests devised a way to let every arm become a sword and every finger become a dagger.

- Karate was developed in Okinawa against the Japanese occupation. The Japanese also had "sword control," and so the Okinawans had to devise a way to bust through their enemies' lacquered bamboo armor with only their bare hands for self-protection. That is why karate, which translates to "way of the empty hand," has the high-powered, straight-arm, board-breaking punches. Karate didn't get to Japan until 1922!

• Filipino stick fighting emerged when the Spaniards took away the natives' edged weapons. The Spaniards could not stop rattan from growing in the jungle. The Filipinos devised a fighting system around these sticks, disguising it as folk-dancing and drum rituals whenever their oppressors were watching. The same motions were used with edged weapons when the rebellions erupted and weapons became available.

• Capoiera was an outgrowth of an Angolan martial art among the slaves in Brazil. While their masters thought they were just dancing, the slaves honed their fighting skills for rebellion.

These and other martial arts were ingenious and effective in their own time and place—and, to a large extent, they remain effective defensive tools today if they are realistically taught as self-defense rather than as a dance or a sport. If they are taught as a dance or a sport, they are not the answer for a woman in the 1990s looking for the skills to be able to defend herself on the streets. Like the Okinawans, the Chinese priests, the Filipinos, and the Brazilian slaves, today's women need to develop their own defensive strategy to meet the challenges of today's dangers.

Like the ancients, women are for the most part forbidden to carry the most efficient weapons of the day, in modern times, firearms. The criminals, of course, still don't care about gun-control laws, just as ancient bandits didn't care about sword-control laws. Women need an unarmed system that can empower them against the dangers of a husband turned abuser or a boyfriend turned date rapist, as well as the potential rapist in an underground parking garage or coming through a bedroom window.

This is what I and my students have, over the years, attempted to do. We take the best from modern Western learning theories, the best from the martial arts—what really can be used in a rape/assault situation—and discard the rest, especially the shame. We exploit a woman's strengths against a male attacker's weaknesses. We simplify the process so that any woman can learn enough in a short period of time to make a real difference if and when—

and to greatly diminish the chances that "if" will become "when." What we have developed is a combination of knowledge about assaults against women, psychological readiness, the ability to tap emotional power, and how to use optimal physical techniques.

Over the past twenty-four years, over four hundred of my women students have prevented assaults by awareness and pyschological deterrence. Of the reported 94 physical fights, in 2 cases the women did not fight but submitted and survived. In the remaining 92 instances, graduates fought back; all 92 defeated their assailants, 52 by knockouts. This is the realization of the Buddhist maxim "truth in action."

As we simply can't train all of you personally, we want to give you the tools to train yourselves.

Chapter One, "A Problem With a Solution," addresses the very real and horrifying problem of sexual and other assaults against women, and seeks a solution. If 33 percent of all rape attempts are successful, what makes the other 67 percent unsuccessful? The answer represents the basis of any woman's survival. This begins with getting in touch with your greatest strength. The most powerful animal in nature is a mother or father with child—and every woman (whether she has children or not) can reach within herself for that strength.

Chapter Two, "Know Your Enemy/Know Yourself," is about how knowledge and understanding can replace fear. This chapter gives a profile—behavioral, psychological, and physical—of the kinds of men who sexually assault women, whether they be strangers, casual acquaintances, or spousal abusers. They all share commonly exposed target areas and other vulnerabilities that allow a woman to successfully defend herself.

Chapter Three, "The Learning Process," includes detailed information about how to physically and psychologically prepare yourself to learn self-defense, and information about how the body and mind can be trained so that self-defense becomes automatic.

Chapter Four, "First Lines of Defense," explores the issue of boundaries, physical and emotional. Women need to know when and how to maintain distance—in an underground parking structure or on a date. A woman's first line of defense is something she already has: her instinctive sense of danger. This chapter details common danger signs and how to respond, and ways to eliminate the power of a male attacker. When physical force is necessary, there are specific target areas to which all men are vulnerable, and there are basic knockout combinations upon which all other self-defense can be built.

Chapter Five, "Winning Combinations," takes physical self-defense to the next level, depicting the most typical attack scenarios and describing precise defensive moves to defeat the attacker, eventually focusing on the woman's advantage when ground-fighting.

Chapter Six, "Ground Escape," takes ground fighting to the next level, demonstrating how you can defend yourself from the most vulnerable positions.

Chapter Seven, "Fighting an Armed Assailant," begins with confronting the fear of weapons and the fear of death in order to fight with total commitment to win. Building on the basic self-defense techniques, this chapter presents the most common armed assaults and gives specific responses to them.

Chapter Eight, "Fighting Multiple Assailants," deals with the gang psychology of cowards. Building on techniques already learned, we will describe how it can be possible, through readiness, technique, and commitment, to fend off more than one attacker at a time.

Chapter Nine, "Expect the Unexpected," examines the legal aspects of self-defense. Police who arrive on crime scenes never expect to find the victim standing over an unconscious attacker—and they will often assume that the victim is the attacker. Furthermore, an attacker has legal rights and can even bring a lawsuit against a victim who fights back. Knowledge about the legal aspects of self-defense is a necessity in modern times.

The last chapter, Chapter Ten—"Believe in Your Power"—offers the inspiration of true stories where women have successfully defended themselves, delivered knockout blows, and then taken their newly discovered power into every aspect of their lives. One such example, however, I will introduce right away. She is my co-instructor and coauthor, Denise Loveday. In the twenty-four years I have taught my system, she is the best co-instructor I've known.

It would be a mistake for any man to try to single-handedly address an audience of women on how to defend themselves. In

our classes, Denise becomes the role model for our students—
and so, in these pages, our voices speak to you together, though
in our introductions and in the stories of our own experiences,
we will speak separately.

—Matt Thomas

Let me begin by thanking Matt for this opportunity. Some
years ago, when I signed up for his self-defense workshop, it was,
quite naturally, out of self-interest. But once I discovered what I
was capable of, and what it meant in terms of my own self-esteem
and sense of independence, I wanted other women—I wanted
every woman—to make the same discovery. Good women and
men, no matter how strong, selfless, caring, and compassionate,
cannot always protect us from bad men and women. We have
to—and can—find a way to do it for ourselves. Violence against
women may be a deep-seated sociological, psychological, and political problem, but until we figure it out and solve it at the
root, the only solution we have right now is our own ability to
defend ourselves.

I grew up in the classic American family complete with a protective father and brothers. Girls didn't fight. Boys did it for
them. Only fathers and brothers can't always be with you.

My senior year in college, I accepted what I thought was a
legitimate modeling job which took me overseas. But after I arrived I was isolated and in essence kidnapped by the people who
had hired me. I was then subjected to mind control and sexual
pressure for the next ten days. I was utterly helpless, surrounded
by men on hilltops holding Uzis, with no means of communicating with the outside world. Using our wits, three of us were finally
able to get ourselves released.

But returning home did not enable me to escape the nightmares or the fear that it could happen again and that I would,
again, be helpless. When I told a close male friend what had
happened, he refused to believe it and said I must have imagined
the whole thing. Perhaps it was too painful for him to cope with.
After his denial of my very real crisis, it became too painful for
me to cope with. I began pretending it had never happened,
which only reinforced my sense of helplessness.

Then I read an article in *People* magazine about Matt Thomas and Model Mugging, and what impressed me the most were the success stories. Of the thousands of women who had studied self-defense using Matt Thomas's methods, only a few hundred had reported being confronted by an attacker. I suspected that the thousands of others weren't merely lucky. They must have learned something that greatly decreased the likelihood that they would be attacked. Of the hundreds of confrontations, only tens of those women had to physically fight. The rest of them had been able to get out of the situation just by using psychological means.

I was compelled to try—to overcome the feeling that I could not take care of myself if anything ever happened again, and, I hoped, to gain some wisdom so that nothing ever would. I can't change the past. I can't go back and undo what was done to me. Yet knowing that I'm no longer powerless is a tremendous help. Perhaps that horrible experience that forced me to learn to protect myself will end up saving my life in the long run.

Reading this book could save yours.

In our classes, we always begin by having students talk about why they have come and what they expect to get out of it. I suggest you explore these questions, and write down your answers. What interested you in this book, and what do you expect to get out of it?

When Matt used to teach a class over several weeks, he would have his students keep journals. That way they could see the changes that took place as their power grew. A journal can be a useful tool for you as you do the exercises in this book. You can help make this your journey by recording it.

—Denise Loveday

CHAPTER ONE

A Problem With a Solution

PROBABLY THE MOST popular defense against personal assaults these days is the Ostrich Defense. It is very simple: 1) Bury your head in the sand. 2) Pretend that bad things won't happen to you. "Hakuna Matata," no worries—what a wonderful way to live.

Unless something bad *does* happen. Then denial is not a very effective defense.

Preparedness, on the other hand, is not only a better defensive strategy, it is also more likely to ensure you peace of mind. Students of ours who have had to defend themselves since taking our course tell us that because they were able to protect themselves, they carry little or no emotional baggage with them from the attack—they are not preoccupied that it will happen again. In other words, "Hakuna Matata" is easier to achieve if you face the potential dangers and do something to prepare yourself.

The fact that you're reading this book means you're concerned about self-defense skills and are willing to do something about it! You are a rarity in the general population.

Joseph Campbell was an astute professor of comparative religion who analyzed common threads in the stories and myths of the world's major cultures. Many others have traveled the path you are on, before. They called it "The Hero's Journey." Think of yourself as a "heroine in training"!

Almost everyone acknowledges that there is evil. Most people simply endure and suffer. Although there is a nobility in martyr-dom, you chose to do something about it.

You have become a wanderer, nay, a seeker. In the caverns of a bookstore, you found your teachers of the "Warrior Way."

You will face your fears to find your love. From love comes your courage to learn, practice, and persevere.

You will confront your internal demons such as anger and despair and release them. It takes a lot of energy to suppress fear, despair, and anger. By releasing these negative emotions, you will have more energy for your joys and passions.

If, or rather when, you face evil, you will resist and succeed. You will save yourself and your loved ones, and possibly prevent other women from becoming victims. The transformation of soci-ety will happen one person at a time.

You are on your own "Hero's Journey" while others still ignore or bemoan the problems.

The problems are very real. However, actual statistics on sexual assault against women are controversial. Police reports show 1 of every 10 American women has been raped. Rape crisis centers report 1 in 3 women. No one is certain how many rapes go unreported.

Whomever you believe, the numbers are frightening. Many women, quite naturally, have reacted by placing great restrictions on themselves—on where and when they go out. We have had women in our workshops say they never go out at night, rarely venture outside their own neighborhood, and feel anger and bitterness at having to live in such fear. Who can blame them? Yet, while we do encourage caution as a major part of preventing assaults, we urge that caution come not from generalized fear but from a knowledge and understanding of and respect for the real dangers.

At no time in human history was there a place that was 100 percent safe. In current Western civilizations, women now enjoy more freedoms than ever before. But your personal safety ulti-mately depends on you.

A better approach for dealing with the realities of danger is to be prepared. Thirty-three percent of all rapes are successful. So what makes the other 67 percent unsuccessful? Research into more than three thousand assaults against women reveals five recurrent factors that seemed to enable women to stop the assault and prevent rape. They are:

1. The drive to survive

2. Formal fighting skills (primarily from one or more of the martial arts)

3. Informal fighting skills (i.e., street fighting)

4. Exploiting a woman's fighting advantage

5. Exploiting a male attacker's vulnerabilities

This represents the foundation of your most effective defense.

The Drive to Survive

All animals have a powerful drive toward self-preservation. In the natural state, when animals are afraid, they freeze, flee, or fight. Humans do the same thing.

A student of ours—let's call her Stacy—once conveyed this story, which illustrates the potential of the human will to survive:

"I was sound asleep in my apartment. It was on the ground floor and it was summer, very hot. I must have conked out without closing a window. I woke up feeling a hand on my mouth, a heavy weight on both hips. A voice in my ear said, 'I'm gonna fuck you and you ain't gonna do shit about it.' I froze.

"Then I tried to get him off me so I could run away, but he was too strong.

"He said something about a knife. I don't know what came over me, but when I heard the word 'knife,' I went berserk. The next thing I knew, I had a lamp in my hand and was smashing it over his head. My legs were kicking wildly.

"I picked up an end table and threw it. He fled.

"I collapsed on the bed, trembling, thinking I was crazy. I could have been killed. Why didn't I just let him rape me and get it over with? I guess I didn't have time to think. I just acted. I sat there crying. If he had come back, I probably would have been defenseless." (This, in fact, was why Stacy wanted to learn formal defensive fighting skills.)

We all have the "killer instinct." Your ancestors, without any formal fighting skills, acted to protect themselves and did so without inhibition. They did it for ten thousand generations. If they hadn't, you wouldn't be here. It is important to recognize that we are killers—that is, we all, no matter what our beliefs, have the potential to kill. We have eyeballs in the front of our heads. We have teeth that are meant for tearing meat. According to neurobiologist Konrad Lorenz in his book *On Aggression,* one-third of the human brain is devoted to survival—which includes readiness for physical combat.

Our society, however, does not encourage women to act on their survival instincts. Females growing up in our society are presented with images of helpless girls having to be rescued by brave men, and these images are often reinforced in people's attitudes. It is a lie. You are no different from those ancestors. You possess the same drive to survive and have the same potential to do great harm and even kill if necessary.

All of you have, or have the potential of, the biological instincts of a "mother with child." No animal in nature is more ferocious. Just ask any forest ranger what he fears most, and she or he will tell you: if you ever see large bear tracks next to small bear tracks, clear the area, because an otherwise docile female bear will attack if she feels her cubs are being threatened. Eighty-seven percent of all bear attacks on humans fall into this category! The maternal (and paternal) protectiveness is true for other mammals, including people. If you have children, we don't need to explain it further.

We once had a middle-aged student say she didn't think she could kill, to which we asked, "What if you saw someone raping your daughter?" Her answer quickly changed. There are many anecdotal stories of women displaying incredible strength—such as lifting cars beneath which their children were pinned. When the adrenaline in your body starts pumping, your strength increases exponentially—and seeing your child in danger is one of the quickest ways to excrete adrenaline. Every woman, whether she has children or not, has this potential. The question is, how can you use it to protect yourself?

The answer is simple. There is a child within all of us. When you are in danger, that inner child is, too. If you are being attacked, so is that inner child. You are the mother and the child. This is why you can be a sensitive, loving, caring person but also have the potential to fight like a female bear and do physical harm to an attacker in order to protect yourself—then go back to being loving, caring, and gentle. You fight not out of hatred for your attacker but out of love for yourself, for the child within you.

Create an image of yourself as a child. Our memories are filled with images, many of them from childhood. Think about your own childhood. What kinds of images come to mind? Which images remind you of your vulnerability, or how easy it was for people to hurt you and how defenseless you were to stop the hurt? An image like that can be called upon when you need to protect yourself. It is an image of red energy, an image that can make you unstoppable.

Here are examples of the images from our memories which we have selected and which we can call upon.

MATT:

When I was nineteen years old, I returned to Japan to find out what had happened to the people I had loved and who had loved me so much when I was a small child. My mother had been disowned by her family for having the son of a white man. My father abandoned us when I was two. My mother did the honorable Japanese ritual of walking with me into the ocean, but returned to shore when I cried. She wanted her own pain to end, but she couldn't kill me. She placed me in an orphanage. When an American family wanted me, in the hope that I'd have a better life, she gave me away. That night she placed her head under the wheels of an oncoming subway train.

As an adult, I have come to terms with the cultural, sociological, and other factors that led to my mother's suicide. But there is still a child within me that has absolutely no understanding of why his mother had to do it, why the person who loved me was so unloved by the world that she had nothing to live for. When I need to become enraged and get my adrenaline pumping—when I need red energy—I think of my mother.

DENISE:

For me, it was just the opposite: I was blessed with a wonderful childhood. I was fearless and loved adventure. I have fond memories of taking off on my own, exploring the woods, a creek, a shopping mall—whatever—and losing track of time. I'm sure I gave my parents numerous heart attacks with all that wandering. The world was MINE! Until, when I was about eight years old, I stopped following my impulses and tried to be what I thought everyone else wanted me to be, a "good girl." I dressed and acted a certain way so that people would like me. I always wore a smile on my face, no matter how sad or angry I was. Now, as an adult and an actress, I'm learning to get back in touch with my emotions and express them. If I need red energy in a confrontation, I think back to that fearless, open little child I once was. No mugger will stop me from defending her!

WRITING EXERCISE*

Bring to mind images of yourself as a child, images of love, joy, pain, fear. Allow your memory to take you on a journey in search of the image that most captures the vulnerability of your childhood.

Write a description of what you see and how it makes you feel. Describe it first from your point of view as a child. Use the first person. Then describe that image from your adult point of view, using the third person.

Formal Fighting Skills

Adrenaline is not enough to ensure your personal safety. But strength without knowledge is an unreliable defense. Remember what Stacy said:

"I collapsed on the bed, trembling, thinking I was crazy. I could have been killed. Why didn't I just let him rape me and get it over with? I guess I didn't have time to think. I just acted. I sat there crying. If he had come back, I probably would have been defenseless."

---

*Really do these! This book needs to be your journey. You need to get emotionally involved with your own past—to discover your old demons as well as your strengths.

Because she was awakened out of sleep, Stacy didn't have time to think about her danger. She'd acted on pure instinct. But had she been awake when the attack began—or had the attacker returned—she might not have responded so effectively. Given sufficient time to think, many victims of attack become terrified and unable to respond in any way. When your body releases adrenaline, there are three possible results: it can put you in a state of temporary paralysis or give you incredible strength and energy to either flee or fight.

Knowing the skills to defend yourself can help ensure that your adrenaline will be channeled into action. Our research into assaults against women found that formal fighting skills did, in part, increase a woman's survival rate. Interestingly, though, it was not the female martial artists who fared the best, but, rather, women who said they just "knew how to fight."

These women tend to be from lower socioeconomic backgrounds where survival, from an early age, is something girls and boys have to take a personal hand in. Most females in our society are raised *not* to fight. "It isn't ladylike." Look around at the culture—at movies, TV shows, books, magazines. Only recently have there been images of strong, able women taking care of themselves. And there remain many more images of weak and helpless women. Things are changing—and we are happy to see more and more students coming to our workshops with an attitude of self-sufficiency and survival. But some women still must make a conscious decision that they are not going to accept the role of damsel in distress.

Informal Fighting Skills

It takes years to master any martial art. On average, a black belt requires four years of study. It can, in fact, take several years just to learn a correct karate punch. Most people do not have that much time, nor can they afford to wait that long to be able to defend themselves. Fortunately, you don't have to. Singer James Brown recorded a song more than a few years ago in which he sings, "I may not know karate, but I do know ca-razy," meaning he knows what he needs to know to take care of himself. Much of what is taught to martial arts students, while being valid and valuable in many aspects of life, does not apply directly to the ability to protect oneself against attack. What you do need to know in order to greatly enhance your chances of defending yourself, you can learn in a relatively short period of time.

For example, though it may take several years to learn the correct way to punch with a fist—so that you don't break your wrist when delivering a blow—the heel-palm strike, using the bottom part of the palm, can be mastered in a matter of minutes and can be quite effective. Karate and kung-fu kicks, usually delivered from a standing position, demand great skill and practice, but almost any woman is capable of delivering a knee to the groin or kicks from the ground position.

Your own drive to survive and a limited amount of fighting skill can be a powerful combination. It allows for unlimited variation to adapt to a given situation. We do not train students to pick up and use beer bottles on their assailants, yet a number of former students who have had to fight did just that. They were not locked into a specific physical response to danger. They knew enough to use whatever was necessary, including but by no means limited to what we had taught them.

Exploiting a Woman's Fighting Advantage

A major component of what we teach is the high/low system of targeting blows. In the martial arts, you are trained in kicks and punches to various parts of your opponent's body. Most of those blows—while making for great motion-picture footage—cannot be counted on to fend off an attacker. A punch to the ribs or the stomach can hurt an assailant, but it will not knock him unconscious, and in some cases, it will only make him mad.

There are two areas of a man's anatomy which are most vulnerable and which give you the greatest opportunity to render him incapacitated. Research into assaults against women finds that women who successfully defended themselves most often did so by hitting their attacker in these two target areas. These two targets are far enough apart that a man cannot simultaneously protect them both. A strong enough heel palm to the nose or a knee to the groin area can incapacitate an attacker. Any solid blow to either area can stun him, allowing you to strike the other target area. In other words, a solid head strike will get his attention above his neck, leaving his groin area completely unprotected. When you knee him in the groin and he leans forward, he's giving you his head as a target.

No matter how muscular your opponent is, chances are he doesn't lift weights with his nose or his groin.

Exploiting a Male Attacker's Vulnerabilities

Another important component of a successful self-defense has to do with the highs and lows of your own positioning. Many fighting systems assume a standing position. This may be fine if you are six feet tall with long arms and a powerful upper body. But most female victims of rape and assault are smaller—often considerably smaller—than their male attackers. Their arms are shorter, they weigh less, and they possess far less upper-body strength. Most of a woman's physical strength is below the waist. If you doubt that, find the nearest gym and see how much weight you can bench-press. Then double it and try that amount with your legs. Men who attack women almost always rely on their upper-body strength. When you use your lower body, you gain a decided advantage.

In order to do that, the focus of your defense is on ground fighting—i.e., defending yourself on the ground. Fighting on the ground, placing your legs between the rest of you and your attacker, immediately exploits your lower-body-strength advantage. Once you are on the ground, 99 percent of the time he will try to use his upper body against your lower body. Because you are in a defensive mode, he has to come to you. Since his arms are almost surely shorter than your legs, you now have the tactical advantage. Ground fighting also prepares you for the more than half of all fights in which the woman is knocked down before she knows what has hit her.

Simple but Powerful

In our classes, we overtrain. We work to prepare students for situations they will probably never have to face—such as what we call the "psycho mugger," the attacker on PCP or some other chemical. Most of our students who have subsequently had to defend themselves have been able to take care of business without having to employ all, or even most, of the techniques we have taught them.

The very first student of ours to subsequently defend herself fell to the ground and front-kicked her assailant in the groin. We always say that the front kick is not as powerful as a side thrust, but in her case, it was enough. Another, more recent example was a woman attacked by four men. She elbowed the first in the chin, missing his nose. But when he slumped to the ground, the other three fled.

What you are about to learn may seem simple. Some of these moves may seem obvious. But do not underestimate their power.

———————————— CHAPTER TWO ————————————

Know Your Enemy/
Know Yourself

DURING THE 1970s, the city of New York launched a public-service advertising campaign to stop impoverished children from playing with the disease-infected rats that occupied their tenements. Hundreds of posters appeared on billboards, in the subways, and on the sides of buildings, showing a photograph of a large rodent above the caption KNOW YOUR ENEMY.

This is good advice. The more you know about and understand your enemy, the less likely you are to become his victim. Likewise, knowing yourself, in terms of your boundaries—in terms of what you consider worth fighting for and not worth fighting for—can go a long way toward preparing you against and preventing physical confrontation.

Although Model Mugging is well known for teaching women effective fighting skills and techniques using an armored assailant, I [Matt] also did careful research on how and why assailants attacked women. Especially informative were the published interviews with convicted rapists. After studying them, I could simulate realistic attacks as a "role-model mugger."

This research was quite a shocking revelation for me. I was only twenty-one years old. I had not been allowed to date in high school because of my parents' strong religious beliefs, so I had learned to become "friends." When my women friends would tell me about "wrestling matches" with their "dates," I knew I was one of the "nice guys." Throughout college, I emphasized platonic friendships rather than having physical relationships with women. I was trying to "save my virginity for my future wife," but my attitude changed in the last quarter of my senior year when I was twenty-two and met the "right" woman. We mutually discovered that sexuality was pleasurable, intimate, and joyous!

So you can imagine how my idealistic and naive views were crushed and then incensed when, as a twenty-one-year-old researcher, I read about what rapists thought about women. How could these men take what is supposed to be the most pleasurable, intimate, and joyous relationship between lovers and turn it into a horror which would then echo in the minds of these women for years afterward? Rape could even prevent some women from ever experiencing the joy!

At the same time, I was caught in a dilemma. How could I teach effectively without realistically simulating an attack? I couldn't. Neither can you. I had to become a woman's worst nightmare in order for her to overcome her fears.

At that point I had already studied the martial arts for eight years. In those classes we have mutual respect for each other; we take turns pretending to be the "bad guy" in order for the "good guy" to practice winning in the dojo, as opposed to discovering the hard way what works and doesn't work on the streets. I easily made the physical transition to become the "attacker" for the self-defense classes. The attack positions sure were different!

Learning to become the verbal attacker was a totally different matter. In reality, in over 80 percent of the rapes reported to the police, the assailants were able to intimidate their victims with verbal threats alone. I was never allowed to swear or say demeaning things when I was growing up. It actually took me a long time to learn to become an effective "garbage-mouth" model mugger.

The hardest transition of all was for me to be simulating an attack on a student and see her mentally go back to her previous real assault to relive the fear and horror. After some of my first classes I would literally be nauseated. However, seeing the women "change their endings" made me focus on the goal of their empowerment rather than on their temporary fear along the way.

The most intense exploration was into my own emotional dark side. It exists in all of us. To deny it only forces its expression in other ways. Distinguishing dark from light and all the shades of gray in between is an ongoing process.

For example, I've trained more than six thousand women during the past twenty-four years. If I hadn't been attracted to some of them, I'd have to check my groin protector to make sure it was doing its job! Some of my students have been attracted to me. I personally don't see positive attraction as a dark side of anyone. Some people might. However, over the years I have found that acting on attractions when so much emotional upheaval is involved is unwise.

At the same time, there have been students whom I've had negative reactions to, and some of my students have had negative reactions to me. What is especially baffling are those students who first "liked me so much" and then "hated me so much"! This brings out the dark side of pain, fear, and anger in everyone that can bounce back and forth, amplifying itself in the process. I choose to acknowledge it and then walk away from those people. Life is too short!

Since you will be learning the physical exercises from this book with a friend, both of you will need to learn to become an attacker as well as a defender. I've learned from my experience in simulating attacks that all kinds of emotions surge! Talk candidly between yourselves. If necessary, talk to qualified therapists! Separate the roleplaying of class and reality. Don't act out any emotions until sufficient time has allowed you to do a reality check.

Through the years, I have learned an enormous amount from my students about their attackers; I did so to better re-create their attacks so that they could act out a different, victorious ending to their experiences. I saw how valuable this sharing among my students was. They talked not only about their encounters and near encounters with rape and assault, but also about their own issues of territory. Rape and assaults against women are not simply acts involving one or more men and one female victim.

We live in a culture in which the boundaries of touch are not always well defined and in which many females grow up confused.

To the insights learned from students we have added our research.

We are neither psychologists nor sociologists, but with the help and inspiration of thousands of students, we have developed some valuable facts about men who assault women—along with some useful tools for exploring the issue of physical boundaries.

Cowards in the Dark

An imaginary enemy is often more frightening than an actual one. When we are children, our greatest fears are often of monsters. As we get older, we may encounter children, sometimes bigger than we are, who are bullies. Looking back with adult eyes, we know those monsters were not real and that the bullies were themselves afraid and insecure and, in most cases, would have been cowards had we stood up to them.

The average rapist is not a huge monster but instead averages five feet eight inches tall and weighs one hundred and fifty pounds.

The average rapist is not a brave and fearless conqueror. He's a coward. All rapists are cowards! Research shows that in half of all rape attempts, any resistance from the woman causes the rapist to run away. The completion rate of rape against a single, unarmed woman is 33 percent. By contrast, the completion rate against a woman armed with a club, knife, or firearm is only 3 percent. The completion rate against a woman armed with a firearm is only 1 percent.

We're not suggesting that every woman carry around a gun, though if all women did, violence against them would probably decline drastically. We point out this statistic to illustrate just how cowardly rapists really are. They are bullies, and we all know what a bully is—an insecure coward. Men who attack women are, like people who make obscene phone calls, cowards in the dark, relying upon your fear. If you don't allow a man the power of intimidation, he may very likely run away to find a more cooperative victim.

Rapists are cowards whether they are street rapists or acquaintance rapists. Fraternity brothers who gang-rape are cowards. Wife beaters are cowards.

Real men don't assault women! Real men don't assault anyone! Cowards, of course, can do great harm. But your fear of them is only useful if it propels you into meaningful action, and your best chance for that is if you respect the threat but also recognize your ability to stand up to it. Like the middle-of-the-night attacker described in the previous chapter, the vast majority of men who assault women neither want nor anticipate any kind of serious resistance.

Fight Out of Love

Acquiring an understanding of men who attack women does not mean sympathizing with them or forgiving their actions. But defending yourself against such men does not require hating them, either. Men who abuse or assault women have more than likely been victims of abuse themselves. Violence and sexual abuse create a vicious cycle in which victims become perpetrators. Some would even argue that no man, if he could look objectively at himself, would want to become a mugger or a rapist.

But whether you agree with this idea or not, there is also a practical reason not to fight out of hatred. An important component of self-defense, as you will discover, is patience—waiting for the right moment to act. Hatred and patience are not always compatible. Also, men will sometimes use sympathy as a weapon—sometimes to lure you in, sometimes to get you to question your hate—which could weaken your defense. Hate as a fighting emotion can be powerful, but love as a fighting emotion is far more powerful.

Your commitment is not to hurt anyone but rather to protect that child within you, whatever it takes. Yes, you will hurt your attacker. Your object is to knock him unconscious. But you're doing it purely as a means of survival. Not because he deserves it. The focus is on you. The focus is on your survival.

Establishing/Reaffirming Boundaries

A recurring issue we find in the research on women who have been the victims of sexual and other assaults—especially those women who have been victimized multiple times—is that of boundaries. All animals have an instinctual sense of how close another animal can come, based upon familiarity and perceived danger. Human society, however, can influence and sometimes corrupt our sense of our boundaries, making it more difficult to defend those boundaries if that becomes necessary.

There are two kinds of boundary violations in nature.

1. *Territorial.* These are battles over a coveted object of some kind. Small children fight territorial battles all the time. Siblings sometimes spend their entire lives locked in territorial battle. Males and females of most species of animal engage in this kind of conflict. They mark their territory and will fight another male or female of the same species if he or she trespasses. Most wars fought throughout human history, including today's urban gang wars, have had at least something to do with a territorial dispute.

2. *Predator/prey.* Predator/prey attacks are also prevalent in nature, usually involving food. A predator hunts down and kills its prey, then eats it. Human varieties of predator/prey, however, also extend to sexual and other conquests. Usually predator/prey attacks are very one-sided. One aggressor, one victim. The victim trying to get away either succeeds in its escape or is devoured.

All too often, men who assault women become predators and the women they victimize are their prey. This makes for a very one-sided fight. But it does not have to be that way. A woman's best chance of survival—of fending off an attack—begins with the mind-set that she is not prey. A woman's best chance for survival begins with establishing any fight as a territorial battle.

There are potentially two benefits from taking this perspective. To begin with, men who attack women—especially (though by no means only) date and acquaintance rapists—are often able to depersonalize their victims. They don't see the woman as human with feelings. She is "a piece of meat." Nothing more. One key to diffusing a situation and avoiding physical violence is to force him to see you as human. Exerting your right to your body can accomplish that, whether that stake is expressed verbally or simply through your body language. But even if it does not—even if the attacker has no conscience at all—insisting upon your territorial right to your body, at all times, can assure that you will be ready to defend it.

Perhaps you have a very clear sense of your boundaries. It never hurts to reaffirm that sense. On the other hand, if you aren't sure about your boundaries, it is time to begin to establish them. Before we provide some exercises we use in our workshops, Denise will share her own personal experience on this issue.

DENISE:

I grew up without much of an appreciation for my body and with much anxiety about sex. When I reached puberty and guys started whistling at me, it made me very uncomfortable. I could sense that to many of them I was a piece of meat, and I didn't like that, but I didn't know what to do about it or how to feel. As I approached adulthood, I couldn't talk to anyone about sex or my own blossoming sexual feelings. I felt alone, confused, fearful, and guilty. As a result, I tended to stay in long-term relationships for their safety, even when such relationships became unsatisfying and unhealthy.

Needless to say, my ordeal overseas as a young adult didn't help me gain a positive image of my physical self—or help me to integrate it with myself as a person.

When I made the commitment to learn self-defense, I also had to make a commitment to establish boundaries. For me, this began with my becoming comfortable with and accepting, and finally and completely owning, my body.

I suggest two writing exercises to help you accomplish this. Maybe you already have a positive image of your body; perhaps you don't have a significant problem around the issue of boundaries. Nevertheless, if you are a woman and you live in this society, you cannot help but be affected by a culture which so often reduces women to their physical characteristics.

WRITING EXERCISE

- Write down exactly how you feel about your body. In detail.
  Be very specific. Try to emphasize the positive while acknowledging the negative. For example:

  *I love my feet. They take me to wonderful places such as the
  mountains for hiking. My knees were injured in a skiing accident,
  but they survived—oh, well, now they can tell me when it's going
  to rain! I like my legs. They are the strongest part of my body. My
  power. Combine my legs with my butt and I have a powerful fighting
  source. While I was growing up, my groin area used to cause me
  a great deal of anxiety. As an adult, though, I have come to love
  my groin and enjoy making love with the right person. Hopefully
  someday a child will be conceived, grow, and be born through there!
  I have a bad back from improperly moving a couch, so I must
  protect my lower back when exercising. My breasts used to be a
  tremendous disappointment. I was ashamed because I was flat-
  chested. But as an adult, I have choices and choose to love me just
  the size that I am now. Moreover, my breasts will someday nourish
  life: my children's lives. I like my hands. They can do amazing
  things. They can create at the computer, give pleasure through massage, or if necessary, defend my life with a heel-palm strike. I used
  to think of my skinny arms as "chicken arms." But with a little
  weight lifting, I've given my arms some shape and strength. They
  may not look like much, but they can become very strong when they
  need to. I like my face and hair. Both have helped me in my acting
  career. I have bad eyes, so I wear contacts. But what I lack in
  vision, my ears make up for in hearing. Finally, I am proud of my
  brain. I love being an intelligent woman. Combine that with what
  I feel is my greatest attribute—my heart—and I am proud and
  thankful to have this body! So this is my body: the good and the
  bad. It gets me through Model Mugging trainings and through
  anything else life throws my way.*

Society is not always clear about boundaries—especially when
it comes to men and women. Rape victims are often accused of
"asking for it." Some men seem to feel that if a woman is attractive enough, she is guilty of making him "lose control." A lot of

women believe this myth, at least to some degree. To combat this lie, I've come up with a set of commandments. Here they are, my inalienable rights as a woman:

1. No one has the right to touch me unless I want him to.

2. I owe no part of my body to anyone.

3. When I say no, when I ask to be left alone, I mean it—and anyone who "kids" around with my body is taking a big risk.

4. If I have to hurt someone in order to protect my body, I can and will do so.

WRITING EXERCISE

Now, write your own set of commandments. If your body is your property, what are your trespassing laws?

As psychologist Geneen Roth, a former student of ours, says, "Women's bodies are not decorations. They are strong, they are powerful, and when violated, they can be deadly."

What's Worth It?

What you are going to learn can enable you to do bodily harm to someone in order to protect yourself. But there is no guarantee that you won't be injured, too. Anytime a person stands up to an attacker, she or he takes on a great risk. Therefore, it is more than a good idea to decide now what is and is not worth a fight. Matt's approach to this question may help put things into perspective.

MATT:

Although I have thirty-two years of martial arts training and can defend myself against unarmed, armed, or multiple assailants, in my personal life I have used my physical martial arts only once.

Over the years, I have been held up three times. All three times I gave the assailant my wallet and my watch. Material possessions are not worth a violent battle, even a battle in which I could have and would have prevailed. In the past three years (since moving to Los Angeles) I have faced three attempted assaults. Each time I've been able to anticipate, avoid, diffuse, or escape the threat by using my head.

I have also been challenged to numerous fights, personally and professionally. Each time I knew I could have defeated my opponent but would have had to retain a lawyer for around $15,000. So-called "honor" and "reputation" are not worth that kind of money. Call me a punk or a coward if you want. I have nothing to prove to myself or to those who love me. Garbage mouth is their problem, not mine.

What if someone insults my children? My wife? My friends?

It has happened. I did not fight over that, because I do not believe that mere words ever justify a physical attack. I don't ever want my children to think that "might makes right." In fact, one of the most important lessons I do want my children—and my students and friends—to learn is one I learned from a Stanford Army ROTC professor. I was with him when an antiwar demonstrator spit on his uniform. This professor was a Green Beret, had black belts in judo and karate, and had endured two tours of duty in Vietnam. I expected him to tear the guy in two. Instead, he just shook his head with sadness. When I asked how he could let someone desecrate his uniform, he replied, "It's only cloth." What he then said affected me profoundly:

"The purpose of a warrior is to preserve the peace. The true pacifist is the samurai who could easily draw his sword and cut his enemy in two, but chooses not to draw it."

What will I fight for?

I will fight to protect my loved ones from physical danger. The closest I ever came to doing that took place one afternoon in a fast-food restaurant. I was standing at the counter with my three-year-old son, about to order, when I noticed a car pull up outside. Out stepped three guys wearing gang attire from a Los Angeles gang. Their shirts were buttoned from the middle to the top, hiding tattoos, making weapons easily accessible. They looked nervous, out of place (we were in northern California, four hundred miles from L.A.).

There was no doubt in my mind what they were about to do: rob the place at gunpoint and possibly discharge their weapons for the hell of it. If I'd seen a way out of there, I would have grabbed my son and left, but the only ways out were through the same door through which two of the three young men were entering or by grabbing my son, leaping over the counter, and making a dash through the kitchen. Carrying a child, I couldn't run as fast as an unencumbered street punk, so I sent my son to a chair behind a ceramic-tiled wall and told him to lie down (bullets will go straight through plaster, but ceramic tile can slow and deform bullets). One of the young men waited by the door; the other approached the counter, not looking at the menu but staring at the cashier.

I stood to the side with my eyes down, waiting for him to draw. The moment he did, I would take him out and use him as a shield, then grab his weapon and neutralize the guy at the door and then the driver. I've done similar hostage-rescue law enforcement simulations in under two seconds.

Fortunately, a UPS driver, eating in the restaurant, had her radio on and a dispatcher asked for her location. It must have sounded to those gang members like a police radio, because they panicked and fled.

But had that not happened, there was no doubt as to what I would do. If I'd had to kill those three young men to ensure my son's safety, I would have done it without hesitation. As committed as I am to avoiding the use of force, I am that committed to using force when it is necessary.

What, to you, is worth fighting over? What is not?

Make two lists.

WRITING EXERCISE

First, list what is worth fighting over—what is worth risking serious injury or death.

Then list what is not worth fighting over.

What you will learn in the coming chapters can enable you to do serious bodily harm to anyone foolish enough to mess with you. With that carries a moral responsibility—to society and to yourself.

—————————— **CHAPTER THREE** ——————————

The Learning Process

THE HUMAN BODY has many joints. As the song goes, "Foot bone connected to the ankle bone, ankle bone connected to the shin bone . . ." and so on. Each connection has a natural—and an unnatural—way of moving. Throwing a ball overhand, for example—as baseball and football players do—is unnatural. As is the tennis serve. That is why baseball pitchers, football quarterbacks, and tennis professionals are prone to shoulder and elbow injuries. It's also one reason that we have been careful to develop this self-defense system in a way that involves only natural body movements. The idea is that you are learning these skills to reduce your chances of being hurt—why risk getting injured in the process? We realize that you can't ask your attacker in real life to wait ten minutes while you warm up—if you pull a muscle kneeing him in the groin, it will be a worthwhile sacrifice. Seriously, though, if you move and stretch every day, the likelihood of injuring yourself in an emergency situation is greatly reduced. Plus you can get many of the side benefits of t'ai chi (yoga synthesized with the state-of-the-art physiology of peak performance) by just moving your body! We use this before we go on an audition, while working on a movie set, or before any athletic activity.

Twelve-Part Warm-Up

To further lessen your chances of injury as you learn and practice these moves, we strongly suggest at least twenty minutes of stretching prior to this—or, for that matter, any—athletic activity.

Put on some soothing music, preferably instrumental, something with a relaxing beat. Get comfortable, in leotards, sweats, whatever feels good and nonconstricting. And warm up in front of a mirror, watching your movements.

If you already have a warm-up with which you are comfortable, you may want to stay with it. If you haven't warmed up or worked out for a long time, we advise consulting a physician before engaging in any strenuous activity. Otherwise, we would suggest following the warm-up exercises we use in our workshops.

As you will see (for reasons explained a little later in this chapter), we do each movement three times, then do its opposite three times.

We begin in a standing position, feet shoulder width apart, one foot slightly ahead of the other, toes pointed straight ahead, knees bent, and pelvis tucked.

Note: NEVER BOUNCE INTO ANY STRETCH and ALWAYS REMEMBER TO BREATHE.

1. Work the Joints

   With hands up, arms in front of you and bent to an angle forty-five-degrees to the floor, elbows almost touching ...

   a) Move your fingers together, one at a time: pinkie to thumb, ring finger to thumb, etc.—until all four fingers are touching. Do that three times. Then do the same thing starting with the index finger and ending with the pinkie.

   b) Rotate your hands, at the wrists, three times in one direction. Then stop. Then rotate at the wrists in the opposite direction three times.

   c) Rotate each forearm, at the elbow, three times in one direction. Then stop. Then rotate each forearm, at the elbow, three times in the opposite direction.

   d) Rotate each arm, at the shoulder, three times in one direction. Then stop. Then rotate each arm, at the shoulder, three times in the opposite direction.

Work the joints

e) Tilt your head down, at the neck. Return upright. Tilt it backward. Return upright. Do this three times. Then turn your head side to side three times. Try to touch your ear to your shoulder, return center, then touch the other ear to the other shoulder. Do this three times. Then gently roll your head in a circle without tilting it backward, three times in each direction.

2. Stretch the Spine and Waist

a) Put the right foot slightly forward, weight on the ball of that foot. Reach up with your right hand; reach down with the left hand. Then reverse hands—left up, right down. Do this three times. Then switch feet (left foot forward, weight on the ball of that foot) and reach up with left, down with right. Then up with right, down with left. Three times. Shake it out.

b) Return feet to the original stance (shoulder width apart, left foot slightly ahead of the other, toes pointed straight ahead,

Waist exercise

knees bent, and pelvis tucked): place your left hand across your torso and on your right hip. Bend your right arm and place your right hand behind your back with the palm facing out. Bending the knees, slowly twist back and to the right. Then face front again and reverse hands (right hand on left hip, left arm bent behind your back) and twist back and to the left. Be sure to keep the knees bent. Repeat this three times. Shake it out. Then switch feet (place the right foot slightly forward) and repeat each side three times. Then shake it out.

c) With both feet parallel and knees bent, bend over as far as you can at the waist. Slowly lift the top half of your body, rolling up one vertebra at a time until you are standing straight up in perfect posture (shoulders roll up and back into the natural set of the scapulae, chest out, head erect). Repeat two more times. Then shake it out.

3. Unlock the Pelvis

Keep both feet parallel, place your hands on your hips, and do each of the following three times:

a) Gently swing your hips from side to side.

b) Tuck the pelvis forward and back.

c) Rotate the pelvis in a circle, clockwise, then counter-clockwise.

4. Warm Up the Ankle, Knee, and Hip Joints
With one hand, balance yourself against a chair or wall. Raise the other hand protecting your face, elbow in, forearm at about a forty-five-degree angle. Bend the left leg slightly.

a) Bend the right leg and raise it up as high as you can, then work the ankle back and forth three times.

b) Rotate the ankle in a circle three times in both directions. Shake it out.

c) Switch feet; repeat with the other ankle.

d) With leg still bent at the knee, rotate your lower leg from the knee joint in a circle: three times in each direction.

e) Switch feet and repeat with other lower leg. Shake it out.

f) From the same position, rotate your entire bent leg from the hip joint in a big circle: three times in each direction. Shake it out.

g) Switch legs; repeat with other leg.

5. Stretch the Spine with Cat Stretches

a) Sit on your lower legs with knees open, back straight.

b) Slowly roll down your spine until you're bent at the waist, face to the ground.

c) Put your arms over your head in front of you.

d) Move forward so that you're lying on your stomach, stretching your arms over your head and pointing your toes.

e) Pull your hands in to the sides of your chest.

f) Push your chest off the ground, tilting your chin toward the ceiling.

Cat stretch

Move forward

Chest off the ground

g) Raise your buttocks up, bringing you on your hands and knees.

h) Arch your back like a cat.

i) Sit back down on your lower legs, keeping your arms stretched over your head, and slowly roll up your spine one vertebra at a time. This should bring you to the original starting position on your lower legs with your back in perfect posture and head erect.

j) Repeat this two more times.

6. Modified Yoga "Plow" Stretch

a) Sit up with your legs bent.

b) Roll back with your feet wide open like a frog's.

c) Stay upside down with your buttocks in the air, knees bent; support your back with your hands.

    d) Stay in this position for thirty seconds (be sure to keep breathing steadily).

    e) Roll down; sit up; breathe.

    f) Repeat this two more times.

7. Rock and Roll

    a) Stay seated on the ground; tuck yourself into a ball.

    b) Put your hands up, protecting your face. Palms out. Elbows pulled in.

    c) Rock back and forth three times.

    d) Roll to the right side, hands still up in front of you, head tucked so that it does not touch the ground.

    e) Roll back to the center for a moment.

    f) Roll to the left side.

    g) Return center.

    h) Roll to each side two more times.

Yoga plow stretch

Rock and roll

i) Repeat this sequence—rock up and back three times; rock from side to side three times—two more times.

8. Isometric Hamstring Stretch

   a) Lie on your back with your right knee bent, right foot planted on the ground.

   b) Slowly raise the left leg; grasp it with both hands behind the knee* or on your calf.

   c) Gently pull it toward your chest.

   d) Stretch it as close to your chest as you can.

   e) Push your leg against your hand for seven seconds.

---

*If you have a difficult time grasping your leg with your hands, put a small towel around your knee and pull on the ends to bring your leg toward your chest.

f) Continue to pull it toward your chest; it should be able to go 15 to 25 percent farther.

g) Push it against your hand again for seven seconds.

h) Relax; shake it out. Repeat with other leg.

9. Isometric Quadriceps Stretch

a) Stand facing a wall and lean slightly against it, supporting yourself with your right hand.

b) Bend your right leg up behind you and grasp the RIGHT foot with your LEFT hand (be sure to keep your left leg slightly bent to maintain balance and prevent hyper-extending your knee).

c) Push the right foot out and behind you against the palm of your left hand for seven seconds; keep the right knee pointed straight down, and you should feel this in the front of the thigh.

d) Shake it out.

e) Repeat with the RIGHT leg and LEFT hand.

f) Shake it out.

g) Switch hands and feet: LEFT leg, RIGHT hand.

h) Repeat the sequence twice.

10. Isometric Groin Stretch

a) Sit on the ground with knees bent and the bottoms of your feet touching each other.

b) Lean your elbows on your knees and gently press down so that knees touch the floor; you should feel the stretch in your groin muscles.

c) When you reach your maximum (the point beyond which you cannot stretch), press UP with your knees and DOWN with your elbows for seven seconds (be sure to exhale and breathe).

d) Continue to push down gently. This time you should be able to go 15 to 25 percent farther.

e) When you reach your maximum, press UP with your knees and DOWN with your elbows for seven seconds.

f) Shake it out.

11. Groin Stretch for Side Thrust Kick

a) Sit on the ground with one knee bent, tucked close to your body.

b) Extend the other leg behind you. Toe flexed.

c) Look over that shoulder.

d) Place both hands in front flat on the ground.

e) Feel the stretch in your groin and buttocks for 20 seconds.

f) Shake it out.

g) Switch legs. Repeat.

12. Any Other Stretches

a) Take a moment and listen to your body.

b) Stretch any muscles that still feel tight.

Groin stretch for side thrust kick

REMEMBER: NEVER BOUNCE INTO ANY STRETCH and AL-
WAYS BREATHE.

Learning Shortcuts

What we said above about natural versus unnatural movements
may also explain why it takes so long to master a fastball or a
tennis serve—since each involves an unnatural movement. With
that in mind, we have been careful to emphasize only natural
body movements. This is why our students are able to learn so
much so quickly (one weekend, about twenty hours) and to retain it for so long (students of ours have used what they've
learned in our workshops as many as eight years later with positive results).

The other component in learning rapidly and permanently
comes from the way in which you practice each skill. Research
into the neurophysiology of learning has given us two very inter-
esting and very useful concepts, which we incorporate into our
program. They are repetitions of three and slow motion.

The third time is the charm. When psychophysiologists studied
how the mind and body work together so they could learn new
motor skills, this is what they discovered: that in most cases, each
time you practice any new skill, you will have improvement from
the first time you try to the second, and from the second to the
third. However, that third try will likely be the best of your current ability—and if you try a fourth time immediately thereafter
(unless you are a world-class athlete), you will probably not im-
prove and you may experience a degradation of learning. By the
fifth and sixth tries, you run the risk of developing bad habits.

Thus, we strongly suggest practicing each move—be it the heel
palm, the knee to the groin, or any of the techniques in this and
coming chapters—three times. Pause and gently shake your arms
and legs after each time. Then, after you have practiced a technique three times, move on to something else. Later, come back
to that same technique for another repetition of three. You will
have a much better chance of improvement.

Speed is relative. Another finding of research on the neuropsy-
chology of learning has to do with speed, coordination, and
memory.

It turns out that your body and mind learn motor coordination skills almost as well in slow motion as at full speed. Since slow motion gives you the opportunity to be more precise than full speed—and is also much less likely to produce pulled muscles or get you out of joint—we have students practice a new technique in slow motion a number of times before trying it at medium speed and then at full speed.

When you are working with a partner, as we will be showing in the photos, make sure the person playing the "attacker" is wearing a groin cup and a face mask of some kind. Matt had his nose broken five times by students who were supposed to be going in slow motion and went fast instead. Now we both wear masks and groin cups even in slow-motion practice when we take on the attacker role.

Most of you won't have a psychological barrier about protecting your face, and most men won't have a psychological barrier about protecting their groin, but this might be the first time you as a woman are being asked to wear a groin cup.

When I [Denise] was asked to wear a groin cup for the first time, I reacted: "No way!" Then I realized that I was going to be hammer-fisted, elbowed, kicked, and kneed in my groin, FULL CONTACT, with my partner driving all the way through! Even in slow motion, I wondered if that itty-bitty piece of plastic would be enough protection!

It is absolutely critical that you practice in very slow motion and that the attacker yield to the motion of the blow, like a slow-motion ballet.

Make sure, however, that you practice each move as a complete punch, kick, or elbow strike. Do not practice half strikes. Follow through all the way. If you can't practice with a partner, try to use targets, such as cushions or punching bags, and give the target a slow but complete strike. If you are ever in a fight, adrenaline will ensure that you fight at full speed and full power, regardless of your practice speed. However, adrenaline may not help you follow through on your punches. That is why there are stories of marital artists who were taught to punch without contact—to swing precision kicks and punches within half an inch of someone's head—who subsequently found themselves in situations in which they had to defend themselves, only to punch and kick without contact.

I [Matt] learned this firsthand in my first "friendly" sparring match against an American boxer. I had three black belts at the time, but all my sparring had been for points. In competition, I was used to pulling punches. The boxer was used to full-force punches, so while I was waving my hands in front of his face, he was taking real swings at me. One connected and I went down. I subsequently studied American boxing and learned a good deal from it—and I'm grateful that I did not have to learn this lesson the hard way, on the streets.

We cannot emphasize enough—and you will hear more about it later in this chapter—that what you do in practice will be what you do when push comes to shove. That is why schools and other places have earthquake and fire drills. As artificial as the drill may seem at the time, those who take it seriously and follow its directions know what to do if there is an emergency, while those who don't take the drill seriously are often the very ones running around like beheaded chickens.

Practice good habits at slow speed.

Inspiration, Not Perfection

Do not expect yourself to perform these moves perfectly the first few times you practice them. Mistakes are all right. They are a part of learning. They are, in fact, essential to learning.

If you ever do have to defend yourself, it is unlikely that you are going to perform these techniques flawlessly. This system, in fact, is designed not to be dependent on exactness for success.

Have fun when you practice. Yes, your reason for wanting these skills is a serious one. Very serious. But learning happens the most when you are relaxed and enjoying yourself. Reward yourself for your hard work. You already have a negative stimulus to motivate you (rape statistics and/or your own past experiences). Give yourself some positive motivation as well. Enjoy the process of learning these techniques and you will learn faster.

We should also mention the inspirational effects of drumbeating. Tests have shown that after a person beats a drum only three times, his or her punches are as much as 25 percent harder than when the individual punches without first beating the drum. In our workshops, we have students beat a drum before they practice-fight. It seems to get the person into the rhythm of combat—which is the reason that so many cultures throughout history have sent off their warriors to the beating of drums. Whether you can do this without disturbing your neighbors is, of course, another matter, but it is a fact worth knowing.

Always Shake It Out

Whenever you practice any self-defense technique or part thereof, be sure to shake out the muscles after each repetition. For example, if you are practicing a heel palm—a punch involving the arms and hands—shake out the shoulders, elbows, and wrists.

Make It Automatic

Keep this and our other practice suggestions in mind as you read the next three chapters and as you practice the techniques therein. Self-defense is not an intellectual activity. Your mind must teach your body so that you can respond without thinking. It should become a reflex. If you have to think, you may not react quickly and decisively out on the street. But you have the potential to make your response automatic. We all do. When you touch a hot plate you don't consciously think, "This is too hot, so I'll put it down." Rather, your hand feels the heat and you drop it immediately.

That is the kind of reflex you need—and can develop—to defend yourself.

CHAPTER FOUR

First Lines of Defense

EFFECTIVE SELF-DEFENSE IS based upon the principle of least resistance. Like water moving downstream, we take the route that is easiest. When water reaches a rock, it gravitates to the place that is least obstructive and flows around it. Keep that image in mind, because that is the goal of self-defense. It's not about fancy-looking flips and kicks. It's about survival—surveying the situation and then utilizing the easiest means of protection available. This can range from recognition and avoidance of danger to escape from danger (what we call "Run Fu") to nonverbal deterrence toward an aggressor (your body language, the way you hold yourself, your attitude) to verbal and physical deterrence and, as the last resort, to self-defense by knockout. Of all these, the most desirable is the first: fast recognition of potential danger and complete avoidance. That is where we begin.

Recognizing Danger: Trusting Your Heart

Fear is a double-edged sword. It can be the greatest threat to survival; it can paralyze when action is needed. But fear is also a warning system, an alert to danger enabling action. This chapter is about conquering fear—preparing to make it work for, not against, you. Knowing and understanding your enemy—the coward in the dark—takes away some of his power. Realizing your own potential strength further diminishes his menace. Rendering him completely powerless means mastering the ways to avoid and, if necessary, defeat him.

That we are animals designed to survive the rigors of nature is a given. For millions of years, our ancestors survived under the most perilous conditions. Our existence today is a testament to their ability to sense danger and react in order to preserve themselves. Their eyes, ears, and sense of smell and touch acted together with intuition like an elaborate alarm system.

Everyone has this capability, but many do not utilize it. Our society does not encourage women (or most men, for that matter) to trust the rapid beating of their hearts, to listen to their keen awareness of danger. A former student, Jenny—a twenty-three-year-old graduate student at the time—epitomized this problem: "I had two brothers and a father who made it very clear that they would always be there to protect me. That I need not worry about taking care of myself—one of them would always be nearby. All I had to do was holler. The problem was, they weren't always there; when I was away at college I was careless. I think I knew it, but deep down I didn't believe anything could really happen to me. One night I was driving home from a party and I knew this car was following me. I guess I felt a little concerned, but I didn't think to do anything. I figured everything would be all right. Well, it wasn't. I should have driven to the police station. I knew where it was. Or to a friend's house at least. But instead, I drove back to my apartment, which had an underground garage. I know it sounds incredibly stupid, but by then I wasn't sure the car was still behind me and I just didn't think anything would happen. When I saw that he was in the garage, I still could have stayed in my car, but I didn't. I let the whole thing happen. I didn't think there was anything I could do to stop it, so I didn't really try. It was like I expected some miracle to save me. When that didn't happen, I just pretended it wasn't happening. I shut off. I went inside myself."

We have heard Jenny's story echoed many times in our classes. And it isn't really surprising. After all, the damsel in distress—whether she is tied to a railroad track or on King Kong's palm—goes way back to early mythology. How many heroines were ever portrayed slaying a dragon? Most mythological heroines are martyrs rather than warriors.

The antidote to all of this brainwashing is simple: the skills and knowledge to take back control of your fate—to give you the confidence to listen to the speeding up of your heartbeat, respond to your sense that something is not right, and recognize it as your signal to act immediately.

Danger Signs

The easiest action, when it is possible, is to sense and respond to danger promptly enough to avoid it altogether. There is nothing shameful in the avoidance of danger. Crossing the street to avoid another person's path might mean offending someone who had no intention of hurting you. But it also could save your life. A woman told me she had been fondled in the middle of a crowded Washington, D.C., Metro car. Afraid to make a scene, she did not resist or say anything—and the man continued to fondle her until the train began to empty out.

The commitment to survival is a commitment you need to make in advance, before you face danger. What is more important to you? Hurting someone's feelings? Being embarrassed because in someone else's eyes you overreacted? Or your own survival? Decide right now. Write it down, think about it, amend it, feel comfortable with it.

Most of what you need to know about sensing danger is already within you. You know intuitively when things are not right and when it is time to act. There are, however, some common danger indicators worth sharing. I've divided them into two categories: behaviors to look for in men you don't know, and those to look for in men you do know.

Men You Don't Know:

- *Proximity.* In all but the smallest of towns, any approach by a stranger is a potentially dangerous situation. There is an accepted social distance in big—and even medium-sized—American cities. The acceptable social distance can vary depending on the culture. It is not considered abnormal for a European man to get very close to a woman he does not know. Asian men in the same situation will typically keep their distance. There are a number of reasons a man might break the imaginary barrier. One possible reason is that he wants to attack.

- ***The eyes.*** Constant staring is an obvious, but often overlooked, clue to potential danger. You can often sense an intense stare even if you aren't looking at the man. Ever been at a party and find yourself turning toward someone who you discover is staring at you? Ever been caught staring when the object of your eyes suddenly turned? This same dynamic can, on the street, be a tip-off to danger.

  Another eye-signal pattern is that of overt looking at your breasts or groin area. Yes, the eyes of normal men do often gravitate toward those areas, but not in a way that is obvious. Any man who will break that social taboo is not only crude. He may also be dangerous.

  The eyes of a stranger can also betray the secrecy of his intentions. When a man looks at a woman with pure sexual attraction, the pupils dilate. When he looks at a woman with violent designs, the pupils dilate and then constrict.

- ***Inappropriate friendliness.*** Situations and circumstances dictate the level of acceptable friendliness. Anything that goes beyond that ought to make you suspicious. Any behavior by a strange man that makes you feel more comfortable may, in fact, be calculated to do so.

- ***Breaking of touch barriers.*** As with social distance, touch barriers vary in different cultures. Europeans tend to be much more liberal about touching. An Italian man, for example, might touch your arm while talking to you. Again, Asian men will not normally touch a woman they do not know at all. North American touching boundaries lie somewhere in between. For example, if you are at a party flirting with a man, some light, nonsexual touching may be acceptable. But not if you are talking to a stranger while waiting for an elevator. The breaking of touch barriers is one way rapists test prospective victims. Contrary to some speculation, most rapists do not want a struggle. The principle of least resistance does not, alas, belong exclusively to you and us. When a strange man approaches you and touches you in any way—

even just a light, seemingly friendly tug on the arm—he may be gauging your resistance or lack thereof.

- *Verbal testing* is another common precursor to a rapist's attack. Almost all women assaulted head-on (not grabbed suddenly) report being verbally tested first; the rapist will ask for favors, then continually escalate his demands. For example, "Can you give me directions? I'm lost." Then: "Can you write that down?" Or, "Show me where that is?" Some of the most notorious serial killers, including Ted Bundy, lured women by seeming to need help with something or by seeming helpless: walking with a cane, wearing an arm in a sling. Also, any man who knocks on your door asking to call the police or an ambulance should be considered a potential assailant. Never let a man you don't know very well into your home for any reason. If you're faced with a cry for help, the safest and smartest thing you can do is to leave the man outside and call 911. (If his plea is legitimate, 911 is the fastest way to get him help; if he has criminal intentions, 911 is the fastest way to get you help.)

- *The smell of danger.* Many rape victims report a specific scent from their attackers—an odor that preceded the assault and which, should they ever smell it coming from another man, will act as a warning. It's a strong ammonialike scent that seems to emerge when a person is that nervous, charged up, and possibly ready to attack.

- *Persistent headlights.* One of the easiest danger signs to detect is that of someone following you in a car. By making yourself more keenly aware of your surroundings and what's in the rearview mirror—especially at night—you can detect if you are being stalked. Our standard of judgment is simple: make three turns. If the same car is still behind you, it isn't coincidence (drive to the nearest police station or other well-lit, well-patrolled building).

MEN YOU DO KNOW:

- The *ammonia smell* and *constricted pupils* should concern you as much on a date as at a late-night bus stop (do not forget that most rapes are committed by a man the victim knows).

- *Gut feeling.* Most women who have been the victim of a date rape or other acquaintance rape say that they sensed that something was not right, but they ignored their own intuition.

- *Overly-physical aggression.* This may sound obvious, but all too often it does not seem so until too late. His insistence, at any moment, on a level of physical affection higher than you want should make you doubt that he will take no for an answer. In fact, a common date-rape scenario is one in which the woman finds herself reluctant to part company in public because she fears embarrassment at having to slam the door on him in front of others. So she puts herself in the much more dangerous situation of being alone and trying to say good night.

Recognizing danger may not enable you to avoid all potential confrontations, but the sooner you realize you are in peril, the more likely you will escape unharmed. A good illustration of this comes from studies of tigers and their predatory habits. The tiger is the most efficient land predator, yet will stalk twenty times before felling his prey. In some parts of Asia, as many as four hundred peasants a year are killed by tigers. But when biologists put masks on the backs of some peasants, then filmed stalking tigers, they found that the tigers, seeing a face on both sides, wanted no part of it. The tigers wanted the weakest and least-suspecting victim. So do most rapists.

The paradox of self-defense is that the more prepared you are to defend yourself, the less likely you will ever have to do it. The better you are able to stand up to danger, the more confidence you will exude; the less attractive you will seem to a rapist.

Water Around a Rock

Before we take you into the specifics of self-defense, a general word about it.

We have combined various martial arts and other self-defense techniques as a deterrent against the most common types of assaults against women—based upon research of thousands of such assaults. But what we teach is much more than specific moves to counter specific attacks. We cannot possibly teach all defenses against all attacks. But just as we learn only twenty-six letters and can use them to make infinite words with which to respond verbally to almost any situation, these self-defense techniques are the building blocks of survival in virtually any threatening situation. We say this now because the most natural thought to have when learning a specific response to a specific challenge is: "But what if he . . . ?" Men who attack women do not use a script. They improvise.

And so do women who successfully defend themselves—like the water in a stream, flowing around rocks and other obstacles, always finding the easiest and most accessible path to its objective.

In an adrenaline state, we tend to fall back on whatever style of physical combat is most familiar to us. Men who have played tackle football, if they aren't trained in any fighting style, will use the tricks of the gridiron, tackling or clipping or clotheslining their foe. Wrestlers and boxers will use these familiar moves.

Although our students learn by practicing the fighting sequences with precision and exactness, each move has the potential for limitless variation. Once mastered, these fighting skills can be improvised upon when necessary. In the heat of battle, when you are fully committed to survival, these techniques can become the basis on which you can defend yourself in almost any situation. As you learn each of these fighting skills, we will describe some of their more common variations. But we could not possibly illustrate them all—and it isn't necessary.

Former students of ours who have subsequently had to defend themselves tell of having used self-defense moves they'd never learned before—from high-heel spiking to ferocious biting to head butting and elbows to the groin. These strikes happened naturally—flowing innately from the sequences these women had learned in our classes. They knew the target areas—second nature—and were able to create variations on a theme. Water around a rock.

This is an ability we all possess if we allow it expression. Ever play-fight with a small child? Grab the arms and the child will kick. Grab the feet and the child will swing her arms. Grab both sets of extremities and the child will shift her weight, bite, elbow, find a way—it's a natural reaction. That many women lose touch with this ability or freeze up when attacked is the result of years of conditioning. But the ability is not gone. Add a powerful set of versatile fighting skills and the confidence of knowing you can use them, and you will, if attacked, find a way to survive.

It all begins with an attitude and a stance. From this stance, many potential attacks can be prevented. If the aggressor is foolish enough to attack, you are ready to explode into action and make him sorry he did.

A Fighting Stance/A Fighting Chance

Unlike the martial arts, real self-defense—whether on the street or in a bedroom—does not always begin from a standing position. Forty percent of women attacked are knocked to the ground before they realize they are being assaulted. But the other 60 percent of assaults do begin as a standing confrontation which may or may not lead to violence. How you respond to this confrontation can determine whether it does or does not. Therefore, self-defense begins with a fighting stance—one designed to potentially diffuse the situation without physical force, and, at the same time, a stance from which you can explode into decisive action.

We call this the "freeze walk" because that is exactly how we learn it. You are walking. Suddenly your heart pounds. You've heard a sound. Someone calling you. Someone coming toward you. You feel that you are in danger. You stop and face the direction of the danger. Do not run unless you know where you're running to and have absolute confidence that you can escape. Many women who run away from an aggressor are caught from behind and tackled, which is not the best position from which to mount a defense. What you want to do is to stand and face the potential attacker in a manner that is most likely to diffuse the situation. If he is open to reason, you want to decrease his aggression. If he is going to attack no matter what, you don't want him prepared for a struggle.

Before we go into detail about the freeze-walk stance, here is a brief overview of what it looks like:

- Feet shoulder width apart

- One foot ahead of the other

- Toes pointed forward

- Knees bent
- Weight on the balls of the feet
- Pelvis tucked
- Arms start at your sides, then swing forward, crossing in front of you to protect your face. Finish with elbows down in front and close together
- Hands up at eye level, protecting the face, waving across each other, palms out
- Arms bent (armpit at a 45-degree angle, elbows at a 90-degree angle)

A closer look at each of these steps:

- Feet shoulder width apart
- One foot in front of the other

Freeze-walk stance

Unless you're into weight lifting, chances are you don't have extraordinarily powerful arms. You can, however, deliver a powerful punch by throwing your body weight behind it. That is why the freeze-walk stance places your feet shoulder width apart with one foot behind the other.

The distance between the feet should be about equivalent to the length of your lower leg—eight to twelve inches. Right-handed women tend to feel most confident with the right foot back; left-handers do likewise with the left foot. It actually doesn't matter. Whatever your right hand learns, the left will—if necessary—be able to replicate. The same is true of the arms and legs.

- Toes pointed forward

Pointing the toes forward is very important. A powerful forward strike requires that your weight be concentrated in the direction of your thrust.

For most women, this is not a problem (Most people walk with their toes pointed forward). But some women have to be aware and make sure the toes are pointed toward the potential attacker. Sufficient practice can ensure this.

- Knees bent

Slightly. Not so much that you feel a strain or that you feel your buttocks pulling you downward. Just enough to give you some added force if you need to thrust forward with a strike.

- Weight on the balls of the feet

The ready position also means having your weight forward. Not so that you are on tiptoes. Your feet remain flat, with about 80 percent of your weight shifted to the balls of your feet, the other 20 percent of your weight on the heels.

If you try this with your feet together and your legs straight, you will probably tip forward. But with one foot in front of the other, balance is not a problem. In fact, in this position you are much more agile; it is much more difficult for someone to push you over.

- Pelvis tucked

Tucking the pelvis gives you even more balance and agility. It also provides more potential power to your upper body.

Models and other women who have been through the rigors of "good posture" say this feels like they're slouching. They replace that image with that of a cat—her back arched, ready to defend herself. Feel your stomach in this position. It should be tighter than usual. That tightening represents the additional power in your punch from that stance.

- Arms start at your sides, then swing inward toward each other, crossing in front of you to protect your face

- Elbows down in front, almost touching each other

The elbows should be no more than a few inches apart. This is important for two reasons. It enables the arms to protect the torso from a forward strike, and bringing the elbows together flexes the pectoral and latissimus muscles into what is called the "pect-lat lock," which greatly increases the power of your punch, should you have to deliver one.

The freeze-walk stance—with elbows in and hands up—is

Arms swing up

a culturally universal sign of nonaggression. It communicates to the potential attacker that you are not offering a challenge, that you are acknowledging and respecting his potential power. It tells him he has nothing to prove. You're not communicating, "Back off, asshole," but rather, I am a human being and have a right to my space. This message can diffuse many situations. If it becomes necessary to fight, this stance gives you two advantages:

1. The opportunity to take him by surprise, since you have given no evidence of resistance.

2. Since he anticipates no fight, his attack will likely become one of grabbing and envelopment, much easier to defend against than if he starts swinging punches at you.

But the same freeze-walk stance with the elbows out accomplishes none of this. In fact, according to studies of animal communication, elbows out is an aggressive fighting posture. By showing any kind of combative stance, your assailant can anticipate resistance and step up his attack.

Keeping the elbows close together also makes the arms a protective shield for your torso and the vital organs therein. In this position, your arms and hands can block punches or absorb the impact of being thrown to the ground or against a wall.

Finally, elbows in readies you to deliver a sudden, solid blow to your attacker. Put your elbows in the ready position, then take one hand and reach over to the opposite pectoral—the muscle area just above the breast. Feel how tight it is. Now, move that elbow outward and feel it get flabby. That muscular tightness is where a good deal of the power in your punch will come from.

- Hands up at eye level protecting the face, waving across each other; armpits bent at a 45-degree angle, elbows at a 90-degree angle

Position your hands as high as if they were holding a pair of binoculars up to your eyes. Palms should be exposed and the hands should move slightly back and forth across each other and your eyes.

The hands protect your face against sudden attack with fists or any other weapon. The waving of your hands is an important part of showing nonaggression—and also breaks eye contact with the potential attacker. This can be very disconcerting for him. Without eye contact, he cannot read you. Breaking eye contact can make him unsure of the situation, confused, possibly even afraid. It can slow his reaction time by as much as one and a half seconds.

Because your hands are approximately twelve inches from your eyes—and because you will have practiced this stance—the effect on you is negligible. In essence, his ability to function is severely impaired, while yours is not—and the potential attacker does not necessarily understand this or know why he is nervous, since you are showing surrender and not resistance.

Waving your hands in front of your face also can draw his attention to your hands and arms, so that if he does attack, he is more likely to grab your hands or wrists—an attack easy to defend against with a thigh to the groin.

Finally, having the hands at eye level locates them perfectly to strike his face. If your hands are too low, his nose will be an upward, rather than a forward, strike. Striking upward is not nearly as powerful as striking forward and can break your wrist.

Scan the Situation

Whenever you are approached in a manner you perceive as threatening, there is always the potential of multiple assailants. When you are under stress, it is common to experience tunnel vision, and you may not see them until it is too late. For this reason, it is crucial to use peripheral vision to assess everything around you. Turn your head to the right, and then the left to gauge the threat.

Talk Is Cheap

The freeze-walk stance is more than a ready position. It's an attitude. When your hands go up, you are establishing your boundaries. No hard feelings, buddy, but you may not come any closer. Every person has—or ought to have—the right to her or his space—a territorial perimeter of at least three feet between strangers unless there is a crowd. Territory is also a right with nonstrangers. That right stands no matter how long you've known him or how much he spent on dinner. You are demanding that right. You don't want to fight, but if you have to, you will go all out.

Men who intimidate and assault women are generally not worth listening to. Their words ought to be given little or no value. And yet 80 percent of all rape victims say they were affected by the garbage the rapist said. There are a number of different kinds of garbage mouth. You need to confront these words now and deflate their power.

The most common garbage mouth is vulgarity, often combined with the threat of force. "Hey, bitch . . . I'm gonna fuck you!" "Slut—you know you want it!" "You fuckin' cunt." And the list goes on. We've all heard these words before—probably thousands of times.

Many of our students find "cunt" one of the most embarrassing words to say. Yet in Norse, Celtic, and Basque language roots, "cuna" means "mother." "Cuneiform" used to mean the mother of writing; "cunning" used to mean motherly wisdom. Some of our students like to think that if someone calls them a cunt, they are really saying "mother." We may not be able to choose what is said to us, but we can choose how we react to it!

We live in a culture in which the saturation of profanity has tended to dilute its power—except when it is directed at you by an aggressor. Then it can be the most horrifying sound.

Garbage mouth may not involve the use of profane language. Yet it may be just as potentially devastating and debilitating. A number of our students who had been victims of rape said that the language which most horrified them was a kind of demented sweet talk. "Hey, mama, I think I'm in love!" and the like. Or any language that objectifies them—that reduces a woman to her body parts—whether pseudocomplimentary or insulting. The underlying message of such talk is that you were put on this earth for his pleasure.

Perhaps the most terrifying garbage mouth is that which comes with familiarity. When a stranger gets personal and knows things about you or utters your name, as in "I've been watching you, Linda," it can confuse and demoralize. A student of ours who happened to be a brown belt in tae kwan do said that she'd been accosted in the ladies' room at a bar several years ago by a man she'd never seen before, and when he said, "I think you looked better with the perm, Tina," she froze up and was unable to call upon her martial arts skills to fend him off. Another common example of garbage mouth with a familiar smell is when someone you know turns ugly. It is a lot harder not to "take something personally" when it is.

Men who attack women very often play psychological games. They want to get under your skin, and push those buttons that will make you feel helpless. Sometimes the sweet talk will seem nice, even innocent. "How are you doing tonight? Having trouble finding your car? I'll escort you. Lotta dangerous people out at this hour." This is no less garbage than a raging accusation or a lewd remark. Your survival depends upon not allowing the trash to impair your ability to react and respond to the situation.

If you feel danger, then whatever he says is garbage—and it cannot touch you unless you allow it. So that it won't, prepare yourself now. Write down every phrase you can think of that would affect you in a confrontation with a man. Say them out loud. Have someone you love and trust say them to your face until the words begin to lose their power—so that when your hands go up in the freeze-walk stance, you can create a wall which no words can penetrate. Just concentrate on your breathing to calm yourself.

Finally, the most perverse yet often the most powerful form of garbage talk from an aggressor is the rapist's lament, his moan. Strange as it may seem, men in this situation will often gain momentary—almost reflexive—sympathy from their victim with an expression of pain, even with tears. "Why are you afraid of me? I'm a human being. I have feelings. I just want to talk to someone!" can be a calculated part of a vicious attack.

These words may be feigned or they may be genuine. It doesn't matter. If you sense danger, then your survival requires that you ignore his plea.

WRITING EXERCISE

DENISE:

In order to be prepared to handle garbage mouth, I suggest a writing exercise. List all the words and expressions that can get to you, that can make your skin crawl or make you tremble. For me, "dumb bitch" or "blondie" is bad, but nothing quite rivals "Hey, cunt!"

To go a step further, give your list to a man you know and trust. Have him cover his mouth with his hands (this acts as a pseudo-mask protecting you from spittle and gives him permission to assume the role of verbal mugger). You calmly stand there in your freeze-walk stance, hands up, concentrating on your breathing while he goes through the list. Have him use emotional content. He should vary the volume and tone of his delivery, speak with intent, and use lewd noises. No matter what he says, don't strike back physically or verbally. Concentrate on your breathing. 3 counts in, 3 counts hold it, 3 counts exhale, 3 counts hold it. It may at first be painful, but after a while the words will begin to lose their power. Eventually the exercise becomes funny when you realize what a limited vocabulary this generic jerk has. But don't laugh. Laughing could make him angry and increase his aggression. Just put this image in your mind: water sliding off a duck's back. Nothing sticks. He can throw this garbage at you, but he cannot make it stick.

One of our former students, a fifty-two-year-old grandmother, was walking home from work one afternoon in Hollywood and saw a man—who appeared to be a pimp—holding a woman—who appeared to be a prostitute—and smashing her face repeatedly into the hood of his car. Unable to get anyone on the street to do anything about it, the grandmother approached the man herself and pleaded with him to stop. The man told her, in graphic and lewd terms, to mind her own business. Since she'd studied Model Mugging and done the exercise preceding, the words didn't phase her. She held her ground and told the man to stop. He threatened to give her more of the same. She put up her hands, and when he attacked, she successfully defended herself and saved the prostitute.

Choose Your Response

The best response in this situation is a rational and not an emotional one. If you are involved in physical confrontation because you got angry, you are no longer a victim; it becomes mutual combat—or, in extreme cases, you become the assailant. The only justification for using physical force is your fear of bodily harm. Therefore, you need to make decisions based on clear thinking about protecting yourself, not about hurting an aggressor.

The clearer your thinking, in fact, the better your chance of survival. One former student found herself approached at a deserted subway stop by a group of men; she started picking her nose in the most grotesque way imaginable, and they left her alone. Because she remained calm, she was able to get out of the situation by using the least resistance. But just as fear can cloud the thinking process, so can anger. Garbage mouth and/ or leering can be enraging—and that rage can propel you if you have to fight—but since avoidance is the best defense, the anger needs to be controlled.

You may, in a confrontation, feel tempted to talk back, to retort. To say, "Fuck you," or something to that effect. This may or may not be a good idea. In rapes and attempted rapes reported to the police where the woman offered resistance, the assailant fled about 50 percent of the time. This number is even higher with date and acquaintance rapists. So a strong "Back off" or "No" can be effective. But if the rapist does not flee, he will likely increase his level of attack and become much more violent. (Never, under any circumstances, say, "Fuck you" to a gun!) There are, in most cases, much more effective methods for talking your way out of a possible confrontation.

Do not attack the self-esteem of the assailant with a challenge, a threat, or an insult. Cowards often feel they have something to prove. Don't fuel his insecurity. Your objective is to convince him to go away. What you say can range from a request—to the effect of "Please leave me alone"—to a firm declaration of your own intentions—"I really need to be going. Good-bye"—to a shouted command—"Get away from me!" No response or anything you say should be more than five words; in an adrenaline state, people are usually unable to remember more than five syllables.

More important than your words is your tone of voice. It should be low-pitched, from the diaphragm, almost a growl. Practice this tone of voice. In any communication, including confrontational situations, only 15 percent is the words themselves. Thirty percent is metacommunication—the tone of voice—and 55 percent is body language. Combining the nonaggressive freeze-walk stance with a low, growling voice can subtly intimidate and confuse your attacker and delay his response time.

You can also slow him down by saying something that catches him off guard and confuses him; make him think, make him wonder. His confusion can turn to uncertainty and fear (more about that in Chapter Six).

For now, when you assume the freeze-walk position, hands in front of your face, arms protecting your torso, you are an island, a fortress. You have nothing to prove. Your objective is singular and simple: self-preservation.

Just Say No

When you thrust into action—and become your attacker's worst nightmare—you will no longer be in a rational thinking mode. You are no longer making decisions; you are acting on reflex. The self-defense skills you are about to learn will, if practiced correctly and sufficiently, take over. In fact, many of our students who have had to use what I've taught them say they remember little of what they've done. A former student called one night to say she had been grabbed from behind on a subway platform and had somehow escaped but couldn't remember how. I [Matt] happened to know some police officers in that city. I called one of them up and asked if there was any report of an assault on that subway platform around that time. My friend said that yes, a man with a long assault record was found unconscious with a broken instep, bruised groin, broken ribs, broken nose. Two years later at a Model Mugging reunion, I put my suit on and mugged her. She promptly stomped on my instep, thighed me in the groin, thighed me in the ribs, and thighed me in the head—and after it was over, she still didn't remember the details of what she had done.

What you practice ahead of time will likely be what you do if and when you have to fight, and there are three common problems you need to prevent ahead of time:

1. **Don't freeze up.** All human beings have a natural potential to freeze up when faced with danger. That is because our ancestors were once the prey of larger and stronger animals, and most of the predators that stalked them detected movement better than they detected shape. Thus, being completely still was a means of survival. Of course, when the predator is another human and you're not hiding, it doesn't make much sense to freeze, but instinct can be a powerful force.

2. **Don't stop breathing.** Related to protective stillness, breathing patterns alter under any stressful condition. Anger, for example, can cause a person to forget to breathe in; sorrow and fear can cause a person to forget to breathe out. Either of these disruptions in breathing during physical combat can make you winded and sap your strength and energy when you need it the most. In extreme cases, you can even become unconscious.

3. **Don't bite your tongue or lip.** A common nervous response pattern to danger is the sucking of the lower lip (a holdover from childhood sucking the nipple and thumb). It is not a good idea when in physical combat. Even the impact of your own punch can cause your teeth to bite down. Biting your lip or tongue may not be the greatest concern, but it can be very painful and thus should be avoided.

The solution to all three of these problems is the same—and it is the answer to your attacker's intentions. One word. "NO." Shout it each time you strike with your hand, your elbow, your lower thigh, or your foot. "NO! NO! NO!" Try shouting NO and holding your breath. You can't do it. Try shouting NO while biting your lip or tongue.

Shouting NO propels you into action. It can also frighten and tense up your attacker. Shouting anything in his face is going to surprise him and slow his reaction time—by as much as a second. It can enhance your strength by psychological focus and it tightens your chest, so that if you are hit there, you can better absorb the blow.

The word must explode from the diaphragm each time. "NO! NO! NO!" Anyone who has studied the martial arts was probably taught a specific word to shout when striking. In karate, for example, many students learn to shout "KIYA" (pronounced KEE-YAHH), which means "shout," or they shout "OS," which is a contraction for "Die a painful death." But your reason for fighting is not because you want to hurt someone. You are fighting to protect yourself, and so the word "no" is the right word. NO, you may not touch me. NO, you may not harm me. NO, you have no right to invade my space or to violate my body. NO, NO, NO! Over the years, as we've seen the collective chanting of our students, the shout of NO has almost taken on a political dynamic—a shared rejection of violence against women.

Two Targets

Before you learn how to hit, you need to know where to hit. This is not about scoring points or looking swift, and it certainly isn't about fighting fair. There is nothing fair about a man attacking you, and so the fairest outcome is you knocking him out, using whatever it takes to survive. Chances are the assailant is bigger and stronger than you. To compensate for that apparent disadvantage, you hit him where he is most vulnerable.

Ever heard a boxing referee address the two fighters at center ring? What does he always tell them? "No hitting below the belt." It isn't the big toes these referees are trying to protect. It's the groin—the testicles. I've watched numerous karate instructors ask beginning students to punch them as hard as they can in the stomach. The result is always a smug, unflinching instructor and one or two students with hurt wrists. You won't ever see a karate instructor tell anyone to kick him in the groin as hard as she can. There is a good reason: no matter how strong or how solid a man is, he can be incapacitated by a forceful blow to the genitals. That is one of your targets.

This is probably not a great revelation to you. We've all heard the phrase, "Kick him in the balls." But you may not appreciate just how disabling a powerful strike to that part of the male anatomy can be. Enough force, well targeted to the testicles, can knock a man (however big and strong the rest of his body may be) unconscious. At the very least, it can knock him silly for several seconds.

Being able to have a profound impact depends, however, upon knowing how and when to deliver the hit. That begins with a precise understanding of this target's location.

You are not aiming at the front of his body but up and under. The idea is to crush the testicles into the pelvic bone—to give his testosterone producers a much-needed vacation.

The other highly vulnerable part of man's body is the nose. Push gently on your own nose and see what little force it takes to cause pain, how easily you can make your eyes tear—easier, in fact, than with tear gas. A forceful strike to the nose can cause blurred vision, bleeding, dizziness, broken bone, and even unconsciousness. By aiming for the nose, at the center of the face, even a miss is likely to strike part of the head and do some damage.

Because the two target areas are at different parts of his body, he cannot defend both at once. So the idea is not to knock him out with one blow, but to keep the barrage going until he is unconscious or decides to get the hell away from you. If he covers his groin, go for the nose; when he guards his face, go for the groin. If he is trying to grab you, chances are he is not doing much defending. He can grab your arms, but that leaves your legs free. He can grab your legs, but then you've got your arms. Like water flowing around a rock, you will become a fighting machine he cannot control, screaming NO! NO! NO!

Simplicity is power. There are two target areas—go after the one that's most accessible.

Heel Palm

From the freeze-walk stance, your first defensive strike is at the upper target, the nose. It's a potentially powerful punch called the heel palm. We teach this punch for several reasons, primarily because it is very easy to learn (whereas learning to fist-punch correctly, so as not to break the wrist or a knuckle, can take years), and also because the positioning of this punch enables you to keep the hands up in a protective position. Therefore, even if your attacker evades the blow, you can still defend anything he might throw.

Feel the very bottom of your palm, the carpal bones. It has more density than any other part of your hand. Put enough power behind the base of the palm and you can break a man's nose.

A former student, a thirteen-year-old girl, used the heel palm to protect her sixteen-year-old sister from a violent, heroin-addict boyfriend. Her first heel palm knocked him down. Her second heel palm knocked him down again. He kept getting up—like a creature from *Night of the Living Dead*—until he noticed the blood all over his face. Then he panicked, held his nose, and ran away.

From freeze walk, the heel palm is a very simple and natural move. If your right foot is back, then lead with the right palm. If your left foot is back, then lead with the left palm. The move is sudden and explosive. The striking arm extends while that side hip thrusts forward, most of the power coming from below the waist, momentum all focused on the attacker's nose. Don't forget to yell, "NO!" with this and every blow. Your other hand stays up—elbow in—protecting your face.

Do not fully extend the arm during this move—that can give you a hyperextended elbow. Jab forward until the elbow is only slightly bent, then pull back into the protective hands-up position. If you keep the elbows in, you can not only deliver a powerful offensive strike but also produce two defensive blocks. The trajectory of your heel-palm strike can deflect any oncoming inside jab to your face—and your pulling back into the guard position can deflect an outside jab to the side of your head.

When practicing this move, be sure you are in the freeze-walk stance with elbows in and hands up. Part of the objective is to knock him backward, away from you. Also, this move can be modified to defend against an attacker with a weapon (Chapter Seven), but only if the hands are up. Make sure as well that your hands remain in a raised position. If you tense them into claws, you may risk a broken knuckle. Be sure to thrust with the hip while you extend the arm. And remember to always shout NO as you strike.

When you strike his nose, imagine your hand driving into his

Heel palm

skull. A good way to practice the heel-palm punch is to kneel on a mat or a firm mattress and alternately right, left heel-palm the surface in repetitions of three, alternating hands and shouting NO with each strike, making sure it is the heel of the palm striking the surface. Remember to "shake it out" after each repetition.

Thigh to the Groin

At the very least, the heel palm will draw the attacker's attention to his head; at the very most, he will be bleeding, teary-eyed, and dizzy. In either case, he will have exposed his other target area. Very often a solid heel palm will send him reeling and cause him to literally present his groin area to you. Your next move is to use the thigh of the leg that is back and drive it forward, under his groin, with the portion of the thigh bone closest to the knee. Shout NO! Then step forward.

Thigh to the groin

Practice this move in slow motion, three times with each leg, shaking it out each time.

Remember, when you step forward on this move, it is with not just the thigh, but the entire body. Keep your hands up because you will put yourself right next to him in order to enable your thigh to drive up and under and through. Like the heel palm, this move is sudden and explosive. Pretend you have a heavy weight on the knee and you are trying to throw it up and off. Done correctly, the thigh to the groin can lift him off the ground, crushing the testicles to the pelvic bone. This can not only save yourself but act as a deterrent against this guy trying to assault anyone in the future.

Numerous graduates of ours have used this technique with great success. One woman was in a very scary situation. On a street in a foreign country, she was grabbed violently by the arm. She spun around and thighed the attacker in the groin. He let go and dropped to the ground—and crawled away.

Even if you miss the groin, a strike into the thigh, hip, or abdomen can still disrupt an attacker's postural stance, create pain and a distraction, and cause him to expose his other target: the nose and head.

These moves are building blocks, so go back and practice the freeze walk into the heel palm, then the step forward with a thigh to the groin. Bring the knee up as high as you can and point your toe down so that you don't pull a hamstring.

Thigh to the Head

If the attacker isn't already laid out on his back or side (the response to which we will cover in the next chapter), then he will, as any man will tell you, bend forward, holding his groin, his head unguarded. You keep moving forward and drive the other thigh into his head. Shout "NO!" There is no specific target on the head—you don't want to rely on fine motor coordination in an adrenaline state. A solid blow to any part of his head can, at this point, knock him out.

Aim for the center of the head but know that any solid blow to his head can knock him down. In fact, a normal person (not hyped up on angel dust or some other drug) can be knocked unconscious by the combination of these three blows. We have designed our self-defense program to overtrain you in case you ever have to protect yourself against a psychotic or drugged or otherwise hyped-up attacker (as a result, more than one woman who has had to use these skills has said that it seemed almost too easy). Even if the attacker is on drugs and isn't affected much by the pain, the mere force of a solid thigh to the head can knock him to the ground. A graduate of ours discovered this first hand, defending herself against an attacker who, she later discovered, was on PCP. "My thigh to the groin didn't seem to hurt him," she reported, "but it got him to his knees. When I thighed him in the head, it didn't seem to phase him at all. Then I thighed him in the head again and he dropped like a sack of potatoes."

As with the thigh to the groin, the thigh to the head is a thrust forward with the entire body that drives the thigh up at his head as if trying to thigh-kick a coconut over a wall.

Practice the thigh to the groin followed by the thigh to the head. It's like a high step with one leg, then a high step with the other. Now practice all three moves, beginning in the freeze-walk position and exploding into the heel palm, thigh to the groin, thigh to the head.

Practice the Entire Sequence

It is important to practice each move and technique individually in order to get a fair amount of precision. But, of course, self-defense is about putting it all together and making it second nature. Therefore, the next step is to practice the entire sequence:

- Freeze-walk stance (feet shoulder width apart; one foot ahead of the other; toes pointed forward; knees bent; weight on the balls of the feet; pelvis tucked; elbows down in front and close together; hands up at eye level, protecting the face, waving across each other; palms out; arms bent; elbows almost touching)

- Scan the situation

- Heel palm to the nose while shouting NO!

- Thigh to the groin while shouting NO!

- Thigh to the head while shouting NO!

Practice the sequence three times, then rest before practicing another three. Keep in mind that the moves you have just learned are a response to a very specific kind of attack—frontal and standing and by an unarmed assailant. The attitude embodied in the freeze-walk stance and focus on high-low target area combinations represent a basis for all other defensive moves.

This combination works against a frontal choke, front slap or punch, front jab or grab. If the assailant grabs your wrists, immediately skip to the next move, thigh to the groin.

In the next chapter you will build on it, learning a defensive response to being grabbed, in various ways, from behind. This will take us into ground-fighting techniques.

In subsequent chapters you will learn how to escape a variety of rape positions, as well as to defend against a knife, club, and gun and against more than one attacker. We will also discuss specific ways to drill, practice, and master these skills.

CHAPTER FIVE

Winning Combinations

WHAT YOU LEARNED in the previous chapter can in many cases be sufficient to fend off a single, unarmed assailant. A former student said, years after taking our workshop:

"I got jumped in my lobby late at night. When the guy came at me I heel-palmed him, gave him one thigh to the groin, and he keeled over. I didn't get to use half of what you taught me."

What you learned in Chapter Four is also the foundation upon which you can add the skills described in this chapter. They will include escapes from front and rear attacks, takedowns, and ground fighting. If there is a moral to this story, it is that it is much better to be overtrained than undertrained.

Although the vast majority of assaults against women are perpetrated by a single, unarmed coward, our self-defense system assumes that you could be attacked by an armed assailant, or more than one assailant, or what we call the psycho mugger—one who is emotionally disturbed or on PCP or crack cocaine or another crazy-making drug.

While visiting a foreign country, a student of ours was followed by three men. She screamed for help, but no one responded. When the guys cornered her, she screamed, "No!" as she heel-palmed the first guy. Blood gushed as he fell backward, hit his head on the pavement, and was knocked out cold. The other two assailants fled.

This chapter is the beginning of that overtraining—taking

physical self-defense to the next level. In it we will offer techniques designed to combat the most common rape and assault scenarios—techniques women have used for all conceivable attacks by a single, unarmed assailant (in subsequent chapters we will provide more techniques against armed and multiple cowards).

The One/two Combination— and the Three/four/five/six . . .

The heel-palm-to-the-nose/thigh-to-the-groin/thigh-to-the-nose combination, while potentially quite effective, is no panacea of self-defense. Real self-defense—in the real world—is not an exact science. Your first strike or kick may or may not hit its target.

If necessary, keep punching and kicking. Repeat the heel palm if you have to. Repeat the thigh to the groin. Let your body take over. Let your eyes find the target and your arms and legs connect with it. An attacker may hit you back and may try to grab you. Keep going at him with full commitment and you will greatly lessen his chances of succeeding. If he grabs your arms, you still have your legs. He cannot hold all four of your limbs at once. It is possible that you could be knocked down. We will deal with that possibility later in this chapter. For now, let us assume the more likely scenario:

That your heel palm/thigh to the groin/thigh to the nose knocks him to the ground.

Like most clichés, there is a great deal of truth to the phrase "The bigger they are, the harder they fall." The adrenaline in your body can make your arms and legs strong enough to put any man of any size on the ground if you come at him with full force and commitment.

But knocking him down does not mean knocking him out. You are not safe until you have rendered the assailant unconscious. He may run away before you are able to finish him off, but you cannot count on that—and, in fact, you must be cautious. An attacker may pretend to run away, only to return and attack again.

He may also fake unconsciousness, or be half conscious. If he is even a little conscious, he is still dangerous. That is why we teach two clear and effective responses to an attacker hitting the ground. They are:

1. Look, assess, yell NO! and get help.

2. Drop to a ground-fighting position.

Look, Assess, and Get Help

If at any point an attacker appears to be unconscious, here are your objectives:

1. Don't try to kill him. This may seem absurd. Here, this guy has just tried to do serious harm and possibly even kill you. Yet, unless killing him is essential to your own survival, it is against the law. Beating someone who is unconscious is against the law and is unnecessary.

2. Make sure, however, that he is unconscious—and not semiconscious or just dazed. A dazed attacker is still potentially very dangerous. If you leave the scene and he's not completely out, he could get up, chase you down, and then you will have to fight all over again.

3. Make sure he is alone—and that you don't get jumped from behind or from the side. Not all multiple assailants attack simultaneously. Some wait in hiding. Furthermore, when you go into the adrenaline state necessary to fend off an attacker, it can cause any of a variety of physiological changes in your body, one of which can be tunnel vision—the losing of your ability to see peripherally, and so it is likely that you have not seen all of what is around you.

Here, then, is the look/assess/get help technique:

• Move away from your attacker. Whether you are standing or on the ground, when your assailant goes limp, put at least three feet of distance between you and him. If you are standing, take a couple of steps back. If you are on the ground, scoot out, moving on the ground in a motion not unlike break dancing, and put at least three feet of distance between you and him.

- Put your hand(s) up into a protective position. Yell LOOK! as you turn at the waist, looking completely around to see if there are any more threats. There could be other assailants or a car coming or any number of unexpected menaces.

- Go to the top of his head, out of arm's reach.

- Look at him. Yell ASSESS!

- Yell NO! The yell should test whether he still poses a threat. If he twitches at all, then he is still conscious and remains a danger to you. For twenty years we used to teach a stomp at the same time, until one of my students, who not only is an attorney but also had been a police reserve officer, asked me how many times I've seen witnesses misinterpret what actually took place. If a witness testified that our student had stomped on the head, that would be excessive force and the student could be charged with a felony. We stopped teaching the stomp immediately.

Practice this move. First the look and assess, then the shout, NO! Do it in slow motion, then speed up in repetitions of three. The shout here serves not only to keep you from biting your tongue but to test his state of consciousness. We have been told by former students who have had to do it that this particular shouted NO carries with it a great deal of satisfaction. It is a triumphant NO! It can also scare off another potential attacker!

Keep the eyes down as you shout—looking directly at the assailant to see if he reacts. If he is semiconscious or faking unconsciousness, the sudden sound will make him move. If he moves, you drop to the ground and kick (more about ground fighting a little later in this chapter).

Obviously, if you are at all unsure of the situation, if there is any doubt in your mind, assume that he is still dangerous and keep after him until you are absolutely sure. You have the right to do whatever is necessary to ensure your safety. That is why your fighting objective is nothing short of knocking him unconscious. If you don't knock him out, he can get up and attack you again.

• If he twitches or makes any movement, drop to the ground and continue fighting. Do not attempt to kick him while standing. You can easily lose your balance and fall, seriously injuring yourself. Kicking from a standing position also enables the assailant to attack your knees, tackling and knocking the wind out of you. Also, if there are witnesses, the sight of you kicking someone on the ground from a standing position can be viewed as excessive force regardless of the truth of the circumstances.

This may seem like an obvious precaution and therefore hardly worth mentioning, but it is extremely important to point out and to practice. In a crisis situation, with the adrenaline pumping, the mind works best when it is on automatic. You are more than likely going to do the thing that is most familiar. Again, if you practice good habits, you will execute them in a crisis.

A good illustration of this is the policeman who was shot during his first shootout when he stood up to reload, placing himself in full view of the armed gunman. Why would he do something that crazy? Simple: because at the firing range he was taught and practiced bad habits. He would crouch to shoot, then stand to reload. When he found himself in the adrenaline rush of a shootout, his body did what it was used to without his mind being able to intervene.

Reaction time is extremely brief. It can cause the mind to defy logic—since logic can take too long to be arrived at in a crisis. So take nothing for granted. Practice looking around, 360 degrees, and if you are ever in this situation, you will more than likely do it automatically.

Do not take the assessment part of self-defense lightly. A student of ours was attacked by four men in a foreign country (one in which victims are commonly blinded during an attack so they cannot identify their assailants). She fought the leader of the gang and knocked him out. The other three fled. She turned and ran in the opposite direction—without doing the look-and-assess pattern. The attacker she had floored regained consciousness, chased her, and within two hundred yards tackled her. She managed to defeat him a second time, but not without serious injury, mostly from being tackled on the pavement.

I [Matt] can tell you from experience what it is like to regain consciousness after being knocked out. In the years it took to fully develop the armor I now wear when simulating assaults against women, I was knocked out nineteen times. Regaining consciousness fills me with a primordial rage, which by now I can control, but which an attacker will use to give him strength and determination against you. This is not something you ever want to confront. Nor do you have to—not if you are sure to practice each and every part of self-defense, including those after the fight.

Take Nothing for Granted

Being prepared means knowing not only when but how to leave the scene.

- Cautiously and swiftly leave the scene. Do so with your guard up, your eyes aware of what is in all directions. Remember, the rush of adrenaline can cause tunnel vision. That means you have to heighten your awareness of your surroundings, not just of people but of other potential dangers, such as traffic.

- Find someone to call for help while you get to a safe place. Who you find and where will, of course, vary depending on the situation. If you are next to your car in an underground parking structure, the safest move may be to get into your car and drive until you find someone to make the call. You can also call when you are safely home—or from your car phone after you've driven to a safe place. If you have been attacked in your own bedroom, you need to get out and find a safe neighbor. If you have any doubts about soliciting the help of a stranger, don't. Move on to safety. Whatever the situation and wherever you are, your priority is to get to safety—not to wait around for the police. The first words you utter to anyone—stranger, neighbor, or friend—should be: "Please call 911!"

  You want to say this with as much calm as you can muster. You are in a heightened state and might otherwise frighten this person whose help you are soliciting (especially if you have just disarmed an attacker of his gun or knife). Also, if you are on the street, approaching a stranger, maintain sufficient distance so as not to intimidate. Let your voice level compensate. What you say after "Please call 911" will depend, of course, on the situation. You want to keep it concise and simple. Something like: "Please call 911! I've been attacked. He's over there . . ." The right words will follow if you begin with "Please call 911!"

Practice this. Run through the entire sequence:

- Freeze-walk stance.
- Scan the situation.
- Heel palm to the nose, yelling NO!
- Thigh to the groin, yelling NO!
- Thigh to the nose, yelling NO!
- Look and assess while in protective stance.
- Shout NO!
- Get help; tell someone to please call 911.

Practice the stop/look/assess/shout NO. Practice getting help after every sequence you practice from here on. Assume that you will win the fight, that you will knock your attacker unconscious, and that you will then have to act fast and rationally afterward. The victory is not in hurting the attacker, it is in protecting yourself and reaching safety. This goal may be dependent upon telling someone, "Please call 911." Always practice these good habits, however simple or basic.

Ground Fighting

As powerful as you may be in an adrenaline state delivering a heel palm to the nose, thigh to the groin, and thigh to the nose, there is certainly no guarantee that you will knock your attacker out in three blows. It has been done many times, but in some

Freeze-walk stance

Heel palm

Thigh to the groin

Preparation

Thigh to the head

cases, what you do on your feet will be only the first part of a successful defense.

The next and probably most important part is ground fighting. This is where real-world self-defense, street fighting, differs dramatically from the martial arts. In the martial arts, being on the ground is a sign of weakness. On the street, being on the ground is actually a greater position of strength.

On the ground, you have a reach advantage. Your lower body is fighting the attacker's upper body. Your legs are longer and stronger than his arms. If you exploit this advantage, you can win the fight, no matter how big and strong he is. That is fortunate, because in some cases—e.g., if you are knocked to the ground before you know what happens, or if you are pounced on while in a supine position—ground fighting is the only fighting you will do.

There are three basic ground kicks you need to defend yourself. They are:

1. the side-thrust kick

2. the front-thrust kick

3. the ax kick

But before you learn these kicks, a word about hitting the ground.

HITTING THE GROUND

Street fighting—whether on the street or in an alcove or in a bedroom—is not pretty or graceful. Nor is it painless. You can expect to get scraped and cut and bruised if you ever have to defend yourself in this way.

Do not be afraid of these injuries, or preoccupied with not getting hurt. Your priority is not an injury-free experience. It is to stay alive and avoid serious harm. If you are cut, scraped, or bruised, these injuries will heal—and during the fight, in an adrenaline state, you probably won't feel them. Do not be tentative. If you are tentative for any reason, you may lack the focus necessary to win. You need to be fully committed to self-defense.

When I [Matt] have had my ribs, fingers, and nose broken

numerous times in class (remember, my students are kicking me full power while in an emotional state), I've continued fighting until the class is done. Adrenaline is powerful!

You might think I'm crazy and there may be some truth to that, but there is a saying in the military: "The price of freedom is the blood of patriots." I don't want to get hurt. Students don't want to get hurt, either, but the odds of a student being hurt in one of my full-contact classes are 1 in 300. The odds of me being hurt are 1 in 50. When guys play tackle football, they get hurt, too. Why do they do it? We both have a goal in mind. For the football players, it's to move a pigskin from one end of the field to another. My aim is to teach women to save their honor and their lives. I will take the risks to accomplish that goal. A student who was injured in class said, "I'd rather be in the emergency room because I was learning to defend myself than because I was raped." The odds of being injured in class are 1 in 300. The odds of being raped are 1 in 3. To not risk learning to defend yourself is actually more dangerous than to do nothing.

In addition, the training you get in class can save your life in other ways.

For example, the safest and most efficient way to get to the ground is as follows:

1. With your hands in a ready position, cross one foot behind you. Bend your knees.

2. Gently sit down.

3. Be sure to keep your hands up in a ready position—allow your legs and butt to absorb the fall; catching yourself with wrists and elbows can cause immediate injury.

4. Roll to your side, ready to kick.

Practice this sequence until it becomes a smooth, integrated roll, so that:

After you have stunned your attacker with a heel palm, thigh to the groin, and thigh to the head, if there is any chance that he is still conscious, you can drop quickly to the ground. He may be dazed. He may be on his knees or his back, or he may be standing. Your thigh to the groin and/or to the head might have

Cross one foot behind

Gently sit down

Roll to your side

missed. Drop to the ground anyway. If you stand and fight, you will probably lose. On your feet, he has the upper-body strength and the reach advantage. On the ground, with what you are about to learn, you can keep him at bay and you can knock him out.

One male student of ours was joining his wife in the shower when he slipped. By tucking, the student avoided hitting his head. It not only saved him from serious injury but also demonstrated the usefulness of martial arts in daily life!

SIDE-THRUST KICK

The most powerful and accurate kicks you can deliver—without years of martial arts training—come when you are on your side. The reasons are simple. Kicking from a standing position requires tremendous practice of stretching and balancing. But in a horizontal position, you can easily employ maximum power and control the direction. Your legs also act as a defense, keeping distance between you and your attacker.

When you hit the ground, get into this position:

- On your side. The bottom leg is bent and tucked under you.

- Up on your forearm.

- Both hands on the ground in front of you, helping you to shift your weight and maintain balance.

If you are on your right side, get up on your right forearm (not elbow!), place both hands on the ground in front and slightly to the right of you, and kick with your left foot. (On your left side, you're up on the left forearm, both hands on the ground in front, slightly to the left, and you kick with your right foot.) Keep your head up and position yourself at such an angle that you see your target as you look over your shoulder.

The kick itself: flex the top foot, bend the knee up to your chest, rotate your hips down as you quickly kick out—at an angle that is almost behind you. Point the toe down and hit with the heel. When it is done correctly, your chest is almost touching the ground as you look over your shoulder at the target.

Get into position and practice the kick in slow motion.

Side-thrust kick

Side-thrust kick

- Make sure to follow through. See your target—the attacker's head, groin, or knees—in your mind and aim for it. Practice this three times on one side, then three times on the other side.

- Make sure to shout NO with each practice kick.

- Make sure that you are looking over your shoulder at the imaginary target. Your power comes from the gluteus muscles in your upper leg and buttocks. You can fully utilize this muscle only when your leg is completely extended.

Think of this kick as something between a side kick and a back kick. Not a push, but a real kick driving all the way through.

If your attacker is moving—on his feet or on his knees—you need to be able to kick from either side. You also need to be able to quickly shift from one side to the other. This is easy. You simply roll from left to right or right to left, shifting your hands so that they trade positions, and you are ready to kick. If the attacker grabs your kicking leg, don't waste energy trying to break free. Simply roll to the other side and kick with your free leg.

Water flowing around an obstacle.

Practice that roll three times.

Then practice three right kicks, roll, three left kicks, roll. Make sure to shout NO. Do it in slow motion. Then at full speed. Aim for different imaginary targets.

FRONT-THRUST KICK

If you end up on your back during a fight and cannot shift to one side for side-thrust kicks, you can use the front-thrust kick. In order to get mobility and power in this kick, it is necessary to sit up with your weight on your forearms as well as on your butt.

The kick itself is a thrusting of one foot after the other—one going high (to the nose), the other going low (to the groin area). The action is as if bicycling in the air. As you kick, point your foot, but also flex your toes so that you will strike with the ball of your foot.

If the attacker has you by one foot, kick up at him with the other. The front-thrust kick does not have as much power as the side thrust, but what it lacks in might, it makes up for in potential speed of repetition and in accuracy.

He cannot protect both target areas at once, so kick high, then

Low front-thrust kick

High front-thrust kick

low, then high, then low. Remember, like water flowing around a rock, you see your opening and you are there with a kick.

The object of the front-thrust kick is to get him away from you. Once that has been accomplished, shift back onto your side and into your more powerful side-thrust kicks.

Practice the front-thrust kick, shouting NO with each kick. See the attacker, see his target areas, and kick high, then low, then high, then low.

The "what if?" we often get at this point is, what if he grabs both feet? A good question—a problem with a solution.

If an attacker grabs both legs, which of your extremities are free? Your hands.

Unless you are attacked by an octopus, he cannot grab all four of your limbs at once. If he has your feet, he's close to you and, with his hands occupied, his head is open for a heel palm; his groin is wide open for a hammer fist, an underhand fist punch with one or two hands.

You keep pounding at his open target, wherever you see it, high or low, face or groin. When he lets go of your legs, resume using them as your primary weapons of defense, seeing the openings and exploiting them. Water around a rock.

Practice the side thrust, three times on each side, shouting NO with each kick, then roll onto your back for the front-thrust kick, three heel palms, then back to the front-thrust kick, then the side-thrust kick three times on each side.

Ax Kick

The last kick we teach is a finishing blow, a very powerful kick you can deliver if the assailant is down but not unconscious. Or if he is trying to get up and attack you again.

The ax kick is simple:

- Same position as the side-thrust kick—on your side, base knee bent and tucked under you, up on that forearm for balance, both hands on the ground in front of you, knee of the top leg slightly bent

- Bring the top leg up and then slam the heel down on your attacker, aiming for the head or groin; the leg should remain slightly bent throughout the entire kick.

Ax kick

Practice this on one side, three times, shouting NO with each kick, then roll to the other side and do three ax kicks with the other foot, shouting NO with each kick.

Practice combinations of the side-thrust kick and the ax kick, shouting NO with each kick. Practice this on each side.

Practice combinations of the side-thrust, ax, and front-thrust kicks. Practice shifting from side to side, shouting NO with each kick. Imagine the attack and experience the variations you can do with these kicks.

There is an even more powerful version of the ax kick, which you can sometimes use. The motion is the same, but this time, wind up into it. Swing the leg out in a circle, up, and then slam it down; again, always keep the leg bent.

The windup action utilizes the strength of the gluteus muscle and can greatly increase the impact of this kick. The direction of the winding action does not matter. You can wind in or out, right or left. Try it both ways. Feel the power in that kick.

Practice the ax kick with a windup. Do three of them with the right leg winding out, then three with the right leg winding in. Be sure to shout NO with each kick. Then roll to the other side and practice three windup ax kicks winding one way, then the other, shouting NO.

Practice the windup ax kick along with the side-thrust kick, the front-thrust kick, and the regular ax kick. Although the windup ax is a more effective strike, it takes more time to deliver and so it may or may not be an option.

Aim the windup ax kick the same way you aim the regular ax—groin and head, high and low. The most profound target you can hit with an ax kick is the rear base of the head; next is the nose. But you need not be that precise. If you miss the head and hit the neck or throat, or miss the groin and hit the abdomen or upper leg of your attacker, you will slow him down; your kick will make an impact.

RISING VICTORIOUSLY

If your attacker has stopped moving and you think he might be unconscious, put your hands up in a ready position. Scoot away on your back—it's kind of a break-dance movement, swiveling 360 degrees so that you can look for possible multiple assailants. Get yourself a safe distance out of your attacker's reach. Look around, saying LOOK! Take a deep breath, then slowly rise.

You have won the fight, you have survived, and that is reason to celebrate, but not now, not yet. You are still in danger. You don't know what is around you, and you cannot be sure yet whether the attacker is unconscious.

At the top of his head ASSESS as described earlier. Shout NO, then find someone and ask them to "please call 911!"

Practice good habits. Try practicing this full sequence:

- Freeze-walk stance.

- Scan the situation.

- Explode into action with a heel palm to the nose.

- Thigh to the groin.
- Thigh to the nose.
- Drop down and use kicking combinations to knock him out.
- Scoot three feet away from him.
- Look while still on the ground.
- Rise up; go three feet from his head.
- Assess, yell NO! and get help: "Call 911!"

Take nothing for granted. Practice good habits and you will more than likely do the right thing if you ever have to defend yourself.

Although ground fighting is the solution to many types of attacks, we have dealt specifically with only one kind: standing, frontal. In the next section we will look at the other common-attack scenario from the standing position: the rear attack.

Defense Against Rear Attack

Cowards who attack women will very often do so without any warning whatsoever. They will hide in waiting and attack at what they consider your most vulnerable moment. This is an unpleasant fact of self-defense, one we must accept and prepare for with caution and readiness instead of fear. If you are alone and feel there is danger, be aware of any place where an attacker might be hiding and avoid a direct path past that spot. Don't be afraid of looking or feeling foolish. It is better to make a fool of yourself than to be made a victim.

Of course, no one has eyes in the back of her head. So we teach defense against attacks from behind.

There are many different ways an attacker will grab and try to subdue. The best defense for all of them is the butt strike.

Butt Strike

No, this is not a means of striking the rear end of the attacker. Rather, it is a means of using your own buttocks as a weapon.

Probably the most common manner in which a male attacker will grab a victim is by wrapping both arms around her upper

Bear hug   Butt strike

body. It can be an overpowering hold, especially if the attacker is tall and very strong. In that position, a victim can often feel helpless. But she is not. In that position, he—the attacker—is vulnerable. He is very vulnerable. He is unprotected and he cannot see your hands. Here is one potentially effective defense.

Imagine that you have been grabbed from behind in a powerful hold. You cannot move to the right or the left. What you can move is your buttocks. You can ram them into his groin. The first step in this sequence, then, is:

• Tuck your head.

• Bend your arms, your hands up, palms out protecting your face.

• Throw your buttocks back into the groin of your attacker.

The motion is a little like the 1970s dance move "the bump." The knees snap to a bending position; the buttocks jut out. This is the last thing an attacker is expecting, and it can knock the wind out of him and cause him great discomfort. It also puts your weight to your very rear and flows into the next step:

• Takedown. Remain in the butt-strike position—head tucked, hands up, elbows in—and let the weight you throw with the butt strike carry you and the attacker falling backward to the ground. Go for the ride. Don't fight it.

The idea is to use the hard ground as a weapon and to use the attacker as your cushion against it. As he hits the ground, his weight and you on top of him will probably make him or both of you turn to one side. Allow him to do so—it will position you for your next move.

These are tricky steps to practice. We do not advise falling backward without a cushion of some kind. Using your practice partner will cushion your fall but will seriously hurt your partner unless he or she is professionally trained, so we ask you NOT to practice the takedown with your partner. You will need a very soft and giving surface, such as a mattress on the floor. Obviously, if you have any back ailments, you may want to simulate the fall without actually falling. In any case, practice these first two steps to the best of your ability without injuring yourself. Shout NO,

Tucked in a ball

tuck your head in, hands up, and throw your butt back, then use the force of your weight to carry you down, backward, to the ground.

At this point the attacker is likely to have been stunned by your butt strike. He is unlikely to be prepared for the fall. He may not be able to brace himself, and the back of his head will take much of the impact of the fall. This fall, with your weight and his, on a hard surface can knock him out. But there is no way of knowing, so don't stop. The rest of this sequence goes like this:

- The hammer fist. This is one of the few times we recommend using a fist punch. Knuckle punching can be hazardous to the bones in your hand, but with a hammer-fist punch, contact is made primarily with the bottom of the fist and is therefore not likely to cause broken knuckles. The punch is simple: make a fist; swing it backward in a natural underhand motion and up into the groin area of the attacker. Obviously, in this position—lying on your side with

Hammer fist to groin

Preparation for . . .

Elbow to the nose

the attacker behind you, also on his side—you aren't going to be able to see where his groin is, but if you swing the fist back and up with full commitment and power, it will find its way to his vulnerable spot. Yell NO!

- Elbow to the nose. Whichever fist you use to hammer-fist, use the other forearm to raise yourself up; then, with the same arm that hammer-fisted, swing the hammer fist in front of you. Bend the elbow and ram it into the attacker's nose. Yell NO! Follow through, turning in toward the attacker.

- Heel palm to the nose. By following through on the elbow to the face, you'll now be on your other side and forearm, facing and looking down at the attacker. The other hand will be in position for a quick, hard, downward heel palm to his nose. Yell NO!

  Your body is turning toward him, so that you lean into the blow. Then, keeping your hands up to protect your face, the heel palm then flows into a . . .

- Thigh to the groin. If you heel-palm with the left hand, your left leg will be in position for a thigh to the groin. Yell NO! If your right hand delivers the heel palm, it will be your right leg. Although you are on the ground, the thigh to the groin is virtually the same motion: bring your knee up toward your chest, taking the attacker's testicles along for the ride.

Heel palm to the nose

- Scoot out and kick. You want to spend as little time as possible within the reach of the attacker. Therefore, after the thigh to the groin, you want to put your own legs between you and him. You accomplish this by spinning on your buttocks or quickly scooting out—again, it is like break dancing.

  You can push yourself to either side; your body will know which way to go. You want enough distance to kick him in the head. You don't want to be more than leg length away. About three feet is good, so that your side-thrust kick can hit him and follow through.

- Let your ground-fighting skills take over. At this point use the side-thrust kick and ax kick—and, if necessary, front-thrust kicks—to finish him off.

Practice this entire sequence. Carefully, again.

- Butt strike.
- Takedown (practice this SLOWLY), curled in a ball.

- Go to one side.

- Hammer fist to the groin.

- Elbow to the nose.

- Turning, facing him.

- Heel palm to the nose.

- Thigh to the groin.

- Spin out.

- Side-thrust kick.

- Combination kicks to the nose and groin.

- Scoot three feet away from him.

- Look.

- Rise; go to top of his head out of arm's reach.

Thigh to the groin

- Assess.

- Yell NO!

- Get help: "Please call 911!"

Remember to shout NO with each blow.

Practice this sequence three times.

One of our students was attacked by four men in a bar. She wheeled with an elbow, missing the nose but hitting the chin of the first guy who grabbed her. He dropped to the ground and the other three fled.

Variations on a Theme

There are a lot of possible variations to this or any other kind of attack. Using these techniques, you can potentially handle them. Remember the image of water flowing around a rock. That is how you fight. That is, in fact, how small children fight (though usually without the technique). Ever tickle or play-wrestle with a child? Grab the child's arms and she will use her feet. Grab his legs and he will use his arms. If a child is small enough, you might be able to grab all four limbs, in which case the child will use his or her teeth, or spit, or find a way to throw an elbow. Somehow the child finds a way, finds an opening.

That child is you, only bigger and stronger!

The techniques you are learning are your weapons—though there is no telling exactly how you may use them if you ever have to. We do not teach women to play dead in an attack, yet we know of women who have used that ploy successfully to survive in extreme circumstances. If there is a will, there is a way.

Standing Release

There are some situations in which you can be grabbed from behind and not be in a good position for a takedown. For example, you are grabbed from behind by the hair, or in a rear choke with his arms extended or with twisting your arm behind you. A butt strike can still daze the attacker, but if his arms are not holding your body, falling backward may not take him with you.

In such situations, you are better off going directly into the elbow to the nose—from a standing position.

- To use your right elbow, step back with the right foot to the seven o'clock position. (Imagine that as you look to the ground you are facing twelve o'clock. Seven o'clock is behind you and to the left.) Your feet will be crossed.

- Your hands simultaneously sweep up into protective stance: hands up, elbows in, palms out.

- Raise up on the balls of your feet to pivot. As you start to pivot, lift your right striking elbow up. (The left hand, elbow in, still protects your face.) Yell NO! as you ram your elbow into his nose. Now, facing him, bring that elbow down which returns you to protective stance with hands up.

- Follow it immediately with a heel palm to his nose, using the left hand. Keep your right hand up to protect your face and continue to attack with thighs to the groin and thighs to the head, shouting NO with each blow.

Practice this entire sequence three times.

- Step back, crossing one foot behind you.
- Arms sweep up.
- Pivot on the balls of your feet.
- Elbow to the nose.
- Bring elbow down and face him in the ready stance.
- Heel palm the nose.
- Thigh to the groin.
- Thigh to the head.
- Look, assess, NO! and get help.

Use this same sequence for the following two variations:

Step back

Pivot

Elbow to the nose

Two Hand Choke from Behind Release

If his arms are fully extended, you may not hit his nose, but you will break his grip and pin his hands under your arms. Follow immediately with a heel palm to the nose, then follow the preceding sequence.

Arm Bar Release

Don't waste energy trying to release your arm. Just as before, bring one foot behind you and spin, using your free arm to elbow him in the nose. Remember, you are water flowing around a rock.

Bear Hug Standing Release

If you are in a bear hug from behind and the butt strike does NOT take you both backward to the ground . . . apply those same moves in a standing position.

- Butt strike straight back, bend your knees, hands up and tuck your head in.

- Shift a hip to the left.

- See the groin. Hammerfist with your right hand up and under his groin.

- His grip should be broken so that you can step back with your right foot to the seven o'clock position, on the balls of your feet and pivot.

- Follow with the right elbow to his nose.

- Face him in stance. Heel palm to nose, thigh to groin, then thigh to head.

- Look, assess, yell NO! and get help.

Release from Rear Choke

This is one of the most dangerous attacks. If the assailant knows what he is doing, you can be unconscious in less than three seconds. Fortunately, most assailants are not well trained.

Getting choked unexpectedly obviously impairs your breathing. No reason to panic, though. You will take charge and be focused.

- Hold your breath. Let's try a simple exercise. Simply hold your breath for ten seconds. No problem! You can do a lot of damage in ten seconds! Heck, you can do a lot of damage in three seconds!

- Thumbless grip. Turn both of your palms in. With your thumbs pressed against the sides of your index fingers (not opposing them), cup both hands over his wrist. Target his wrist that chokes your throat. Use your pects and lats to do a chin-up as you . . .

Thumbless grip pinning his wrist

Butt strike

- Pin his wrist to your shoulder (or waist—the problem with teaching the pin to the waist in class is that it will cause the instructor's hands to pull down over the student's breast. Due to personal boundary issues, we don't teach the waist pin, even if it is more effective.)

- Butt strike. You already know this. This should give you some breathing room.

- Step way out to one o'clock. Imagine that as you look to the ground you are facing twelve o'clock. With your left foot, step as far as you can toward one o'clock.

- On the balls of your feet, pivot 180 degrees to the right. Keep his wrist pinned to your shoulder. This will use your leg muscles against his arm. This will break his wrist and snap his elbow. Practice this move extremely slowly.

- Left foot steps alongside his right foot. This will rebreak both his wrist and elbow.

Step to one o'clock

- Right thigh to groin. This should double him over.

- Left step to make up any distance.

- Right thigh to nose.

Although this might seem complicated in writing, it is like a dance . . . a dance of life for you. It might not ever be taught at Arthur Murray's.

- Hold your breath.

- Thumbless grip pinning his wrist to your shoulder.

- Butt strike.

- Left foot steps to one o'clock.

- 180-degree pivot to right.

- Left step forward to side of his foot.

- Right thigh to the groin.

- Left step forward.

- Right thigh to the nose.

- Look, assess, yell NO! Call 911.

If the assailant is left-handed (only 15 percent of the population is left-handed), the same technique can result in a throw which also breaks the elbow and wrist.

This is also the precursor to a defense against a knife at the throat.

Practicing being attacked from behind is scary and can cause tremendous fear reactions. Remember to breathe. Now let's find a way to deal with this fear.

Left foot steps alongside his right

Find the Courage

In order to believe in yourself and trust your own power and will to survive, it is helpful to get in touch with the inspiration for your courage. We have all, in our lives, benefited from the courage of others—especially those who love us—and we have all been courageous.

Here are some examples.

MATT:

I owe my life to my mother in more ways than one. She did what she had to do to ensure my survival, at the expense of her own. First she took me to an orphanage so that I would be fed (being Eurasian, I would have been shunned in Japanese society). When she saw the opportunity to have me adopted by an American family, as painful as that was, she acted on it. It took tremendous love, sacrifice, and courage for her to give me away. But she is just one example of a person whose courage has touched me.

Great courage need not involve the risk of one's life. We had a student whose brother revealed his homosexuality to the family, and dispite a harsh reaction from their father, by continuing to live a life of love, he eventually brought the family closer together.

WRITING EXERCISE

What acts of courage have most touched you?

Write them down. Describe these acts of courage and the people who performed them.

Write down the most courageous thing or things you have ever done. Describe how you felt and where you feel that courage came from.

You are your own greatest inspiration.

With enough courage, you can overcome even the most harrowing situations—some of which will be addressed in the next three chapters.

CHAPTER SIX

Ground Escape

It is very important for you to approach this chapter with your courage. This might trigger emotions associated with previous horrible experiences, or it may be the stuff of primeval nightmares for you.

With few exceptions in nature, when the predator has the prey on the ground, it's all over for the prey. But you do not have to be prey. You are a predator, too! You have eyes in the front of your head. You have eyeteeth for tearing meat, but more importantly, you have the most effective weapon of all, the human brain!

You can also emulate one of the fighting strategies of the big cats. Often a smaller tiger will roll backward from the charge of a bigger tiger and then use its powerful hind legs to disembowel the tiger on top. You, too, have the use of your legs.

Appreciate what you have.

WRITING EXERCISE

Acknowledge your fear about being pinned by an unarmed assailant. Write down which fears being pinned brings up in you! Leave some space after each fear so that by the end of this chapter you can go back and write down how you can transform that fear into a problem with a solution. Some of these fears are well founded. Some might be an extrapolation of being overpowered in "play" by a father, older brother, boyfriend, etc. Some of these fears might come from television or movies. Take time to identify the sources of your fears.

Then immediately write down your hopes and the step-by-step approach you will take to realizing these hopes.

Don't give in to the temptation to skip your writing and just start reading this chapter. Make this journey your own! If this chapter gets too scary, refer back to your hopes!

Realize that in the past, you didn't have enough tools to take care of yourself. Now you will get the tools you need.

First of all, your fears are well founded. In more than 40 percent of all rapes and attempted rapes, the victim is knocked to the ground before she knows what has hit her—or is attacked while lying down. Very few rapes take place when women are standing up. For many women, being pinned to the ground is their worst nightmare. Yet, with courage, commitment, and the right techniques, you can protect yourself.

You could start kicking right away, and many women have and prevented being pinned, but it's important to take the worst-case scenarios and teach you how to deal with them. By removing your fear of them, you can think more clearly to choose when to fight.

Let's imagine that you are pinned. A coward on top of you is not invincible. He may be stronger than you. He may have more physical size. But he is not a mother protecting either her real child or her inner child.

When you are on your back, the would-be rapist on top is actually quite vulnerable. He is vulnerable because, in order to accomplish his objective, he must expose his target areas. He has to use his hands to control you, but he also needs them to perform the rape. He may not expose himself right away. That is why your survival may depend on clear thinking, and on patience. If you panic, you may miss your opportunity or try to fight back too soon. It is understandable to panic in any of the situations we are going to describe. Understandable, but avoidable. With enough courage, you won't panic.

There are four basic ground-start rape positions:

1. On your back

2. Oral copulation, weight forward

3. Oral copulation, weight backward

4. On your stomach

Each position has its own problems and each problem has a solution.

Release from On-the-Back Pin

When women have used this technique in real attack situations, they were startled how easy it was and how far they threw their assailant. Often it was clear off the bed or couch, and the guy had to deal with dropping from a height. In one case, the woman threw the guy into a wall; he was knocked out after his head hit first the wall and then the ground.

Being pinned on your back is a position associated with weakness, powerlessness. But it doesn't have to be. From that position you can throw an attacker off, take charge, and successfully defend yourself. Most likely the attacker will straddle your waist, using his weight to hold your lower body, his hands to control your upper body.

He may, in this position, seem to dominate, but he is not invincible. He can be thrown. Whether he is sitting on your waist or lying on your stomach, he can be thrown off. Here is how:

- Bring one knee, preferably your right one, up slowly, planting that foot while keeping the other leg extended. This gives you leverage and power. Do this slowly and easily. He cannot see behind him and should have no idea you are getting your leg into position as the launching pad of your hip rocket!

- Bring your arms in. There are two variations to this move. If he straddles your waist and swings at your face, let your arms take the blow by quickly placing your wrists on the

Bring one knee up

Thrust with your hip

bony ridge above your temples and bringing your elbows together. Your face is protected while your arms are in a pect-lat lock position. If he's lying between your legs while pinning your hands to either side of you, bring them in as much as possible. Remember, when your arms are in tight you can deliver a more powerful blow.

Since your hands pose no obvious threat in that position, there is a chance that an attacker will not resist this movement. In fact, he may put your arms there, since it brings his closer in and gives him the illusion of more control.

- Wait for the opening. Don't attack while his weight rests on all four limbs. You would just waste your energy. He has to move a hand, whether to hit you, take off your clothing, or unzip himself. Now he's in an unstable, tripod position, his weight supported by three limbs. If he lies between your legs, he's a tripod again. Now he's unbalanced. Now it's time to explode!

- Thrust upward with the hip. If you brought up the right knee, thrust with your right hip to the left; if you raised the left knee, thrust with the left hip to the right. If you made a mistake and brought both knees up, you will trap him between your legs and have a hard time throwing him off! Use only one leg and keep that foot planted throughout the entire toss!

This is a very natural movement, the kind of thing you might do if you were play-wrestling someone. But with one knee bent and with your adrenaline exploding into action, it can be very powerful.

Practice this move. Do it in slow motion. Imagine you are pinned in a rape situation. Take your time. Feel yourself thinking clearly, not succumbing to your fear. The key is to wait for him to get between your legs, then:

- Bring one leg up.

- Plant the foot.

- Arms in.

- And explode with your hip thrust.

- Shout NO as you thrust.

Repeat this sequence three times.

When you have thrown him off, you do not retreat. You attack. Finish him off:

- Heel palm to the nose. Your upward hip thrust should flow right into this. The pect-lat lock will give it power.

- Thigh to the groin. Your top leg should be in a good position for this.

- Scoot out and kick. Side-thrust kicks and ax kicks to the head and groin.

    If he grabs you so that you cannot scoot out, keep attacking the target areas with heel palms and knees to the groin, holding your hands up and elbows in to protect your face. Keep going at him until you believe he is unconscious. Then:

- Look, assess, yell NO! and get help.

    Practice this entire sequence. Begin on your back, bring one leg up, bending at the knee, plant that foot, thrust upward, then attack. Shout NO with the thrust and with each blow. Practice it in slow motion three times with your partner. Then practice in medium speed without your partner.

STACK THE DECK

"This all seems too easy" is a typical reaction of students. "What if he weighs two hundred fifty pounds and is very strong?"

The answer is that, with your adrenaline pumping and the right leverage, you may still be able to throw an attacker off in this manner. In class, I [Matt] weigh 260 pounds in my padded, protective suit. We have had ten-year-old girls who weigh less than 100 pounds toss me off with ease after their initial "Ugh! Are you heavy!"

However, you don't want to take the chance that you won't have enough power to thrust him off. Therefore, be aware of your every advantage and be prepared to use each one.

This brings us back to the need for great courage, the courage to be patient, to allow time to pass while you are pinned on your back. Rape is a power game, and part of your power comes from waiting for your opening. Openings come in one of two ways:

1. His needs: the ones he creates.

2. Distractions: the ones you create.

- Exploiting his needs. It may seem absurd to be contemplating the needs of a rapist. His needs are an affront to humanity. But his needs are also a key to your self-defense. This is one reason we advise students to fight out of self-love, not out of hatred for the rapist. Hatred can blind you to his point of view, and his point of view is one of the keys to your survival. What does the assailant need to do to achieve his objective? In all likelihood, he needs to a) disrobe you, b) disrobe himself, c) position himself and you, and d) maintain concentration and focus.

    These needs can translate to your opportunities:

a) Disrobing you. Chances are he has to remove your clothes, possibly his own. In order to do this, he must release your hands and use his.

b) Disrobing himself. He may even have to struggle with his own zipper. Any such action can create an opening—a moment for action.

Of course, there is no guarantee of this. One student of ours had previously been attacked by a man in a trench coat with nothing on underneath it—and she was in bed at the time with very little on herself.

One unfortunate fact about men who attack women is that, since they are rarely caught and even less likely to be prosecuted, they become better and better at what they do. The average rapist who is caught has usually raped seventeen women. On the other hand, he gets used to a passive victim and isn't likely to be expecting a fight. He may also demand that you take your clothes off. How you respond to that will depend on the situation, and there are no absolutes. But if you're calm, you can choose the best response. You may choose to be cooperative until the moment you explode into self-defense.

Or you may act disoriented, terrified, unable to move—then suddenly explode and attack. In any case, even if he has managed to remove clothing without creating an opening, he has other concerns—which creates opportunities for you.

c) Positioning. The assailant cannot complete his rape without getting between your legs. In order to do so, he again gives up much of his power and control. Of course, he may try to minimize his vulnerability by putting both of your hands above your head and leaning on your wrists, leaving one of his hands free to push your legs apart. But in this position, his weight is already shifted forward. He is probably off-balance—so that if he weighs 250 pounds or more, that weight will help carry him off you. And in this position he has no way of protecting his target areas.

You are not helpless. In fact, if you see things from the attacker's perspective, you will realize that you present a tremendous amount of problems for him.

d) Concentration and focus. The rapist has a lot to think about—beyond the logistics of what he is trying to do to you. He doesn't want to be seen or caught. If he is going to succeed, he must concentrate and stay focused on his objective. One reason many rapists use garbage mouth may be that it not only gives them power but keeps them focused on their objective. If you can disturb his concentration and blur his focus, you will have a much better chance of surviving, and of preventing the rape. He may seem to have taken control of the situation, but you need not allow that. If you don't panic, you can choose your reaction and maintain control.

- Here are some examples of distraction techniques we have learned from our students who have survived past assault attempts:

a) Exaggerate the fear. Being assaulted may well be the most frightening thing that ever happens to a person. Yet if you are confident of your ability to survive, you can pretend to be much more afraid than you are. One former student tells of pretending to be paralyzed, unable to move, and giving off what she described as a "catatonic squeak." This left her attacker completely unprepared for her sudden attack.

b) General disorientation. Your confusion can make him confused. In fact, anything you say to an attacker can be a distraction. A statement like, "Where am I? Who are you?" Or the pretense of knowing the attacker or knowing something about him. All these things can make him think, make him lose a degree of concentration. In situations of date or acquaintance rape, you can use your familiarity with the person to say something you know will throw him off guard. For example, call him by the name of someone you both know.

c) Bizarre statements and questions. Related to the above, this technique, especially used right before you explode into your defense, can throw an attacker completely off guard. One former student, in a potential acquaintance-rape situation, announced, "I'm from the snake people!" Her attacker never knew what hit him.

Another strategy is to pretend to go along with the guy. While he is sexually distracted, you can easily launch your attack.

An attacker doesn't know what is real and what is calculated. By choosing your response, you make an attacker think. You have taken charge of the situation. In fact, although this technique is more likely to be useful in these kinds of attacks (and in defense against armed assailants, next chapter), distracting an attacker can work in a variety of scenarios, including assaults from a standing position. Anything that can distract the attacker from what he is doing gives you an advantage, and no attacker is immune to distraction.

As a martial arts fighter, I [Matt] am very good. Bud Winter (Olympic coach), Ed Parker (the "father of American karate"), and Grand Master Chumakov (SOMBO is the most widely practiced martial art in the world, since it was the military and police official hand-to-hand combat system for the former USSR) all said I have some of the fastest hands they've ever seen. I'm an experienced tournament fighter. I've studied over twenty different martial arts styles and have four different multiple-degree black belts. I was sparring one of my female martial arts students who was a beginning white belt. She pulled open her *ghi* top, exposing her bra. The Macy's lingerie ads in the daily paper are more revealing, but I was flabbergasted. She easily punched me in the face, then kicked me in the groin. Distraction works on everyone!

Release from Oral-Copulation Position

These are, perhaps, the most horrible positions in which an attacker can put you: on your back, him straddling your chest, pinning your arms with his knees, and trying to force his genitals into your mouth.

While an obvious defense is the use of teeth once his objective has been accomplished, it is not necessary to wait for that. Also, if your bite is not fatal, he is in a position to take retaliation on your head with potentially serious consequences. Finally, a bite is ill-advised due to the risk of HIV (at least 10 percent of the prison population and 10 percent of all IV drug users test positive for the HIV virus).

A better defense is to use his vulnerability against him. Again, his concentration is on one part of your body. He has no idea what your legs are doing. Therein lies his great weakness. Either the attacker is leaning forward or he has his weight behind him. Here is how, in each case, to exploit his position:

1. **Weight Forward**
    In this position, your arms are pinned against your sides, but with his main focus elsewhere, there should be room to maneuver.

Here, then, is that escape:

- Bend both knees and plant both feet on the ground.

- Quickly bring both hands together to make a double fist. Do NOT interlock fingers, otherwise you might break them. Also, this is NOT like a volleyball serve in which you use your thumbs. You want to strike with the fronts (the knuckles) of your fists.

- Simultaneously drive forward with your whole body, lifting your hips off the floor while striking his testicles with your double fist. Your aim is to force the assailant to lurch forward—hopefully smashing his head into the wall or headboard.

Hands make a double fist

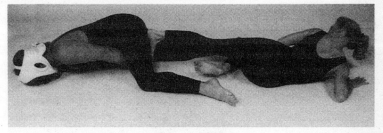

Spin and kick

- Spin around and kick. Use combinations of the side-thrust kick, front-thrust kick, and ax kick to knock him out.

2. Weight Backward
   In this position, your arms are pinned beneath his legs and he is sitting on your chest.

Here is the escape from that position:

- Wait for him to sit up!

- Swiftly swing both legs up, wide like a frog's.

- Hook both feet around his shoulders. Actually, given the angle, it is your two heels that could converge and lock on the assailant's head.
  This is a quick, sudden move. In order to do this, you use the momentum of swinging your legs wide and up so that your buttocks leave the ground and the weight of your entire body can be used.

- Pull backward on his head, neck, or shoulders. This will yank him downward, jerking his neck and slamming his head back on the mattress, ground, or pavement. At the same time, it brings you up until you are sitting upright.
  And it will leave his groin area completely unprotected.

- Elbow to the groin. Now that you are sitting up and his groin is literally in your lap, elbow him in the groin.

- Scoot and ax-kick. At this point, you should be able to scoot

Hook your feet

away from him. In all likelihood the assailant will be keeled over now. Ax-kick him in the groin to be sure!

- Knock him out. Use combinations of side-thrust kicks and ax kicks to his head and groin until you are sure he is unconscious.

   Then look, assess, yell NO! and get help.

Practice these moves. Do them in slow motion. Unless you and your training partner are trained professionals, we do not advise training with each other on this particular technique. Even in slow motion, this can be extremely dangerous. Imagine you are pinned at the chest and hands. Use a large pillow or other soft object to give yourself an idea of size and distance. Imagine the assailant preparing to force himself into your mouth. See your opening. Perhaps it is when he unzips. Or perhaps he has already done so and it is time to act.

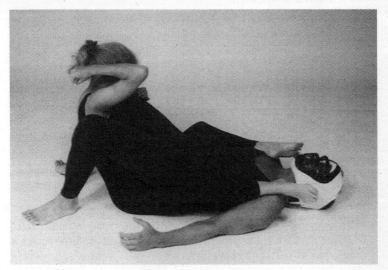

Elbow to the groin

- Bring both legs up, wide like a frog's.

- Hook them around his shoulders, neck, or head.

- Slam him down, bringing yourself into a sitting position.

- Elbow his groin.

- Scoot away.

- Ax-kick his groin.

- Side-thrust his head.

- Look, assess, yell NO! Please call 911!

Shout NO with each strike. Practice it three times.

Men who assault women can be on PCP or other drugs which can enable them to endure great pain. Once you have initiated a fight, he may try to hurt you back.

This technique is the crowd pleaser at graduations. What looks like the worst horrible pin is swiftly turned around, the mugger is thoroughly trashed, and the student arises victorious.

Release from On-the-Stomach Pin

Another common rape position is the stomach pin, with the assailant on your back.

It can be the most frightening, since you cannot see your attacker and do not know what he might do. But as vulnerable as you might be, so is the attacker. Just as you cannot see him, he cannot see all that you are doing. Whether he is sitting or lying on your back, he can be thrown off and defeated. Here is how:

- Wait until he is between your legs. If he intends to rape or sodomize you, he will have to spread your legs and put himself somewhere between your knees.

- Bring one knee up (toward your stomach) like a lizard; plant that foot, keeping the other leg straight. This move is similar to the first move in release from a back pin, except

Bring one knee up

that because you are on your stomach, the knee goes in instead of up.

As in the back-pin release, the raised leg and planted foot provide you with leverage and power. Bring the leg up slowly, as though you are trying to get comfortable. It is unlikely he will suspect anything. You could also do this suddenly as part of your explosion of power!

- Bring your arms in as much as he will allow you in a pect-lat lock position. This, again, is the same move you did on your back—and it is done for the same reason. In this case, however, it should be easier to accomplish, since your arms are hidden from his view.

- Rotate your hips. If you brought up the right knee, thrust to the left; if you raised the left knee, thrust to the right.

As with the back-pin release, this thrust should come naturally. The body knows the easiest and most effective way to shake off an unwanted weight. But with one knee bent and with your adrenaline flowing, you can throw more weight than you might have thought possible.

Practice this move. Do it in slow motion. Imagine you are pinned on your stomach. His weight is on your back and he is holding your arms. Feel yourself thinking clearly, not succumbing to your fear.

- Bring the leg up

- Plant that foot

- Arms in

- Explode

Shout NO as you thrust him off. Do it three times.

The motion of throwing the assailant off your back flows directly into the next move, just like the takedown release:

Plant the foot   **Elbow to the nose**

- Elbow to the nose. As you throw him off, follow with the elbow.

As your momentum carries you, turn in and smash his nose with your elbow, keeping your other hand up in protective position.

After the elbow, bring that arm down so that you can support your weight on your forearm and be facing him for a heel palm to the nose. Your protective hand attacks.

- Thigh to the groin. After heel-palming him in the nose, bring that hand back to protect your face and knee him in the groin.

Don't stay close to the attacker any longer than is necessary. You want to put some distance—and your most powerful weapons—between you. Thus, your next move is:

- Scoot out and kick. Use combinations of side-thrust kicks, ax kicks, and, if necessary, front-thrust kicks.

Practice this entire sequence:

- Begin on your stomach.

- Bring one leg up like a lizard; plant that foot, keeping the other leg straight.

- Then throw him off.

- Follow that immediately with an elbow to the nose.

- You now face him; heel-palm his nose with the other hand.

- Give him a thigh to the groin.

- Shout NO with each strike and kick.

- Scoot out and kick.

- Look, assess, yell NO! Please call 911!

If it seems to you that the techniques in this chapter are all very similar, you are correct. In fact, the more similarity you see and feel, the more reason you have to be confident about what you are learning. This similarity is what enables you to learn so much so quickly and to be able to adapt what you have learned to a wide variety of circumstances.

Variations on a Theme

The four rape positions in this chapter are the most common, but they are not the only ones. Nor do all rape attempts follow any kind of predictable succession. Sometimes the victim is knocked to the ground and must start fighting immediately. In other cases, a rapist may attack while the victim is on her stomach, then turn her over; or attack when she is on her back and turn her onto her stomach; or start in either of these positions and move into the oral-copulation position.

As long as you remain committed to your survival, you can adapt—even if the techniques you've learned seem to be thwarted. For example, if during a release from the oral-copulation position the assailant suddenly leans forward so that you cannot wrap your legs around his neck.

You have already committed to the release. There is no turning back. What do you do? You go for the target areas. Use your feet and hands. Make something happen.

In throwing an attacker off, he may not fall where you antici-pate he will.

It doesn't matter. If you are fully committed to your survival, your elbow and heel palm will find him, and your legs will put up a barrier and be in the position to finish him off.

An attacker might start hitting you before you are set to throw him off. If that happens, act. Get your hands up, if possible, find his target areas, strike back, do what is necessary to maneuver your legs between you and him, and kick. You will find a way.

The Will to Survive: Fully Committed

Street fighting is an inexact science. Real self-defense is messy. The only guarantee is that if you are fully committed to self-preservation, then your will to survive can become stronger than any assailant's will to harm you. An attacker can never be as committed to his objective as you can be to yours. His target is an abstract. Even in cases of date rape, the victim is somewhat arbitrary. A nonperson, an object. What you are fighting for is the most important thing to you, the most important thing to any person: life itself.

Where your safety and survival are at stake, overtraining is the only rational training. Yes, men who attack women are cowards and therefore, ultimately, very weak. But that weakness can be masked by drugs or alcohol. An attacker on PCP (angel dust) or crack cocaine or various amphetamines can withstand a tremendous number of punches and kicks and keep coming. Psychologically disturbed people can be equally dogged. Such attackers are the exception. But you want to—and can—be ready for anything. Therefore, assume that anyone who attacks you might be mentally unstable or hyped up on drugs. Don't expect him to fall after one kick, or even after three or four. Keep kicking until the assailant is knocked out.

Being fully committed means feeling no sympathy for your attacker. This may seem heartless. Perhaps he had a rough life, was sexually abused himself. If he's your ex-boyfriend, you may know firsthand of his personal hardships. We can consider these factors when discussing rapists as a social problem and trying to invent solutions. But if you are fighting for your life, you must resist feeling anything toward the attacker. It may seem absurd that anyone would feel pity in these circumstances, but some rapists use sympathy as a trick. Be prepared. Once you embark on self-defense, carry it through to its conclusion. If the assailant apologizes, do not pay any attention. If he says something pitiful, like, "I only wanted to talk to you," or, "Nobody ever loved me," ignore him. Once he crosses your boundary, once he forces you to commit to self-defense, there is no turning back. If he gets up and runs away, we don't suggest chasing him. But don't trust him, either. Assume that he might run around the block and try to jump you again. Take nothing for granted and focus on survival.

Being fully committed also means fighting through the pain. With your adrenaline pumping, it is unlikely that you will feel much pain during the fight—students who have subsequently had to defend themselves have been badly bruised; had ribs, arms, and wrists broken; have been beaten in the face and head, and worse. And all were still able to fight back successfully (one woman did not realize she had broken her wrist in her self-defense until two days later!). But there is no guarantee that, should you have to defend yourself, you won't feel some pain. It is rare that anyone successfully defends herself without sustaining some injury. Hopefully, injuries will be minor, but fear of being hurt can prevent you from a successful defense. This may be a life-and-death situation. There is no time to stop and think.

White Energy, Red Energy

In Chapter One we discussed the idea of fighting out of love rather than hate; of picturing the child within you as your child, the concept of you as mother of yourself; and of being willing to risk your life as mother to protect your child. We call this white energy, the adrenaline boost we get from an image of love and courage—inspiration, something that helps us focus on what is worth fighting for, what is worth fighting to preserve.

We also discussed red energy, another powerful source of power, inspired by images of great pain, of loss, of anger, that come from love.

We suggested that you write about your own experience, something that can give you red energy. Read what you wrote and remember that image. Place it clearly and vividly in a part in your memory from which you can recall it, instantly, anytime you need to.

Think of people you love. Imagine that you are saving them as you practice heel palming, one hand after the other, in succession on a mat or a punching bag. Imagine your red-energy images and hit the target again. End with the white-energy images. Do the same with your kicks.

Always start with the white energy, then think of the red and end on the white. We want to surround the killer who takes life with the warrior who preserves life.

Now practice the moves in this chapter in the same way and as you move on to the next chapter, defense against an armed assailant.

Finally, go back to your journal, read over your fears about being pinned by an unarmed assailant, and transform each fear into a problem with a solution.

CHAPTER SEVEN

Fighting an Armed Assailant

ALTHOUGH 75 PERCENT of assaults against women reported to the police and 95 percent of the rapes reported to rape crisis centers are committed by single, unarmed assailants, we have to prepare to face an armed attacker. Perhaps it is the most cowardly of men who attack women who rely upon guns, knives, and other weapons. It may be small consolation to know that the man pointing a lethal weapon at you is a coward, but it is an important piece of information, a reminder that you can remove his security—figuratively and literally—if you refuse to be made helpless.

Defeating an armed attacker begins with confronting your fear of that weapon. It is intelligent to be afraid of a gun, knife, or other weapon. The key, then, is not to be unconcerned, but rather to care so much about living that you won't let the sight of a weapon distract you from your objective: survival.

This chapter will begin with the subject of our mortality and how facing that is a key to fighting an armed attacker. We will also provide an overview of this kind of self-defense, including a discussion of the psychology of the armed attacker. Then we will demonstrate how the skills you learned in the previous three chapters can be adapted to fend off someone with a gun, knife, or blunt object.

Why even try to fight? you may wonder. Statistically, it may seem the best response to the crisis since only about 1 in 200 rapes is a rape/murder (1 in 500 or 600 if you consider how many rapes go unreported to the police). We have even had students who opted to risk a fight and survived. You've probably heard this advice, perhaps by a policeman, that if a man tries to rape you, lie still and let him get it over with so that he doesn't hurt you.

But ask the same police officer if he would allow himself to be raped. The answer will be an emphatic, "Hell no!"

Then consider how many women are *injured* during a rape—about one out of *four*, many of them seriously. Consider that rape itself is an injury, a very serious one (though, to our horror, it is not counted as such in crime statistics).

Finally, and perhaps most important, ask yourself if you should trust your safety or your life to a rapist.

We need to make our own choices of when to endure and when to fight with everything we have. *The Survivors* by Terrence DuPres is an inspiring example of people faced with that decision. It's about the heroism of endurance in Hitler's and Stalin's concentration camps. The people described in this book had all physical control of their lives stripped away, but survived due to the strength of their spirits. For us, there may come a time when we decide we must fight, and it is when we fight with passion that we can overcome overwhelming odds. In real life, women who have taken only our basics class successfully defeated assailants armed with clubs, knives, and guns.

Two graduates of the basics class were attacked by two assailants, one armed with a gun, the other with a knife. One student took the gun away, then threatened the knife bearer, who then fled.

Another student was attacked by a former lover with a hunting knife. She dropped to the ground and started kicking. She kicked him full power in the groin with no visible effect. The guy had just been released from a mental hospital and was on a number of medications. He made ten or more attempts to stab her, but by kicking she got only two "cat scratches" on her legs. Finally, in desperation, she grabbed the knife by the blade. (In class we teach to go for the wrist instead, but she did the best she could!) Although her hand was severely cut, she did not feel the pain because of her adrenaline state. She yanked the knife out of his hands. Since they were on a boat dock, she then kicked the knife into the water. While he was distracted by the falling knife she kicked him into the water. Moments later, the sheriff arrived. It took four deputies to pin him down. They told her that Model Mugging had given her a second chance to live.

Life and Death

Most women attacked with a weapon are not killed. Most victims of gunshots do not die. These may not be very comforting statistics. The idea of being stabbed or shot or clubbed is horrible, perhaps even inconceivable, to most of us. It's something we would never want to contemplate. But only by confronting these fears can we be confident of our ability to survive such attacks—and with such confidence, you will probably reduce the chances of ever being attacked in this fashion.

In a life-and-death situation, if you stop to think about your course of action, you greatly reduce your chances of survival. The average criminal can pull the trigger of a gun in seven-tenths of a second. It does not take much longer to move the blade of a knife or strike with a blunt object. That is why you need to utilize the energy of an adrenaline rush while maintaining your ability to stay calm and think. You must be able to quickly assess the danger and react. If, for example, you have a knife at your throat, it is crucial that you recognize not only where the blade is but also where the attacker's hand is. Otherwise, rather than moving the blade away, you could actually cause it to cut your own throat. Similarly, if you are held up with a gun and you are with someone, you have to be clear thinking enough to assess the location of your companion so that if you need to knock the wrist of the gun-holder (who may, in the process, pull the trigger), you won't knock it in the direction of a friend or loved one.

If you fight someone with a gun, knife, or other weapon, there is a good chance that you will be hurt. You may be bludgeoned, stabbed, or shot. But being bludgeoned, stabbed, or shot does not mean that you are dead. Your skull is very hard. It can withstand a lot of beating. So can the rest of your body. Only a fraction of people who are cut with a knife die. Less than 10 percent of all Americans who are shot die from those gunshot wounds. Nor does being shot or stabbed mean the fight is over. It does not mean you have lost. It does not mean that you are dead or will die—your survival depends upon continuing to defend yourself.

Though most of us associate being stabbed or shot with death or severe injury, there is a big difference between being stabbed once or twice and being stabbed twenty-five times. There is a big difference between being shot once or clubbed once and being shot or clubbed multiple times. And that difference often has to do with whether or not the victim fights back.

One of the key aspects of police training is to get recruits to understand this. Often, in simulation exercises, they will be shot and then throw their hands up in defeat. They have to be trained that if they are conscious, they are not dead, and that if they are not dead, then the battle is not over.

Most of us also associate attacks with weapons as being excruciatingly painful. That is not necessarily true. In fact, most of the pain of such wounds is delayed. Most people who have been shot or stabbed report that they don't feel much of anything right away. They are too busy trying to survive. Actually, many victims are not aware that they have been shot or stabbed, nor can they tell what kind of injury they have sustained. At least initially, some gunshots, stabs, and clubbings can feel a lot alike. A dull, heavy pain. Like a hard punch. A feeling you can fight through. A feeling to make your adrenaline flow, to let you know it is time to save yourself. In an adrenaline state, you can withstand a great deal. Former students—and even some instructors—report sustaining broken arms, broken wrists, and concussions, and fighting through the wounds until they defeat the assailant. They felt pain, but it was not so overwhelming that they could not fight. In fact, the pain made them want to defeat the attacker even more.

WRITING EXERCISE

One of the things we have students do before they learn the actual techniques of defense against an armed assailant is to write their own eulogy and epitaph.

We do this for several reasons.

1. It helps us begin to face our own mortality by dealing in a positive way with the fact that life is not forever. It can end at any time. This is a fact each of us knows and most of us push as far away from our consciousness as possible.

2. By writing down all the good things we have accomplished and stood for in our lives, by recognizing our contribution to friends, family, community, and society, we get in touch with the most important reasons to defend ourselves and stay alive.

Very simply, what we mean by a eulogy is something you would like to be said about you if you were to die tomorrow. What you are about and what your life has been about. The epitaph is a brief inscription you would want on your tombstone or on a monument in your memory.

Here is an example of a eulogy and epitaph written by Denise:

DENISE'S EULOGY:

You are all gathered here this afternoon in the Grand Teton Mountains of Wyoming to honor the life and passing of Denise. She didn't want this to be a sad affair, and that is why she chose to have you, her family and friends, meet at her favorite place. She also hopes the hiking boots issued to everyone fit comfortably, making the hike up to this grassy meadow by the glacier lake overlooking the snowcapped peaks an experience you will always remember.

Denise loved dogs and children, so if you have a dog or a couple of children with you, don't force them to be still or be quiet. Let them run and play in the mountains. Denise would be running right with them.

Since Denise's career revolved around the arts, we've provided supplies to inspire you: paper and pens to write poetry and funny skits, paints and canvas to capture this incredible scenery, guitars and other instruments to create music, movie and still cameras to photograph the wildlife. Have fun. Be creative!

And when you get hungry after hiking or creating, stuff yourselves on the gourmet Italian food—Denise's favorite. After dinner eat lots of s'mores. Denise would have!

As the sun goes down and the bright stars light up the night sky, sit around the campfire with the one you love. That is what life is about.

So celebrate living. Don't mourn the passing of Denise. Because that is what she did, just passed from one adventure to the next!

Epitaph: "On to her next adventure."

Write your own eulogy. Write down what you would like said about you. Read it aloud to yourself. You may want to share it with a friend. Save it and revise it as time goes by. It may seem a morbid idea, but most of our students find this exercise helpful in building and maintaining their resolve to survive. It by no means makes them fearless, but it does help them become less terrified of death at the hands of a man with a weapon.

Guns, Knives, Clubs

Throughout history, human beings have survived in part because of their ability to use weapons. The natural world can be beautiful, but it can also be brutal. Death is everywhere and the food chain is perpetual. Humans have never had the physical strength or speed to survive and prosper in the animal kingdom by those traits alone. What we've had and still have are our brains—our ability to think—and our thumbs—our ability to construct, grab, and use tools, which include weapons for hunting and defense.

So at least from a historical perspective, weapons can be considered an advancement. If not for them, we would not be alive today. Our species would be keeping dinosaurs company in the ground. Weapons have also enabled small, frail people to defend themselves against larger and stronger people. In fact, although we do not specifically teach techniques of doing so in our basics courses, grabbing a makeshift weapon is a valid means of self-defense. If you are in the frame of mind to survive, a lamp, a glass bottle, and many other objects can become tools to that end. One former student reported using her three-inch high heels in her defense. When a man tried to molest her as she was leaving work, she stomped his foot, impaling it with her shoe. She ran away like Cinderella with one slipper; he fainted, hit his head on the pavement, and was knocked out.

It is no secret that weapons have also provided destructive and evil people with a means to dominate, oppress, and do great harm.

In fact, as we discussed in the Introduction, most of the martial arts were developed in order to enable an oppressed group of people, a group without access to the weapon of the day, to defend themselves against an oppressor who did have weapons.

We, too, have been disarmed by our "authorities." In many parts of our country, the law-abiding citizen is not allowed to "bear arms," even though this was guaranteed in the Bill of Rights (the militia in those days was every able-bodied male citizen over the age of seventeen, who was required to bring his own "assault musket" to defend the common good). Today many people feel that we are at war with a growing criminal element— which is heavily armed and which cannot be disarmed through gun-control laws. (Proof? Is cocaine illegal? Yes. Is cocaine available to the criminals? Yes. If guns were illegal, would they still be available to the criminals? Yes . . . I rest my case.) Yet despite the Bill of Rights, most of us can no longer bear arms against the evil.

However, every year over two million citizens defend themselves by pointing a firearm at a criminal. In 13 out of 14 such instances reported to the police, the criminal flees without shots being fired.

Fact: the completion rate of rape against an unarmed woman is 33 percent.

Fact: the completion rate of rape against a woman defending herself with a firearm is one percent.

And so it would be a misrepresentation, in our view, to advise women about self-defense without advising them to consider and reconsider the laws that keep you from being able to use the most efficient weapons of the day. Should you buy a gun and get trained in its proper and safe use? That is a difficult decision for many women to make. There are numerous issues to consider, so we suggest you read *Armed and Female* by Paxton Quigley, who is a former student of ours and who used to be "antigun" until she interviewed women who wouldn't be alive if they hadn't defended themselves.

Of course, even those of us who do decide to arm ourselves can still only legally do so in our own home, where 40 percent of assaults against women take place. We certainly would never advocate breaking the law, so when an armed criminal approaches us, we must fight with our empty hands and feet, like in the days of old . . . Karate . . . the way of the empty fist.

Of course, today the weapons carried by the bad guys are slightly different from those faced by Chinese priests or Japanese peasants or Okinawans. You are unlikely to be confronted by a man with a sword or, for that matter, with a bow and arrow. That is why an unarmed defense against an armed assailant requires creating a new fighting system to combat the weapons that are now out there. These weapons fall into three categories:

1. *Blunt striking objects.* This is anything heavy enough to wield, such as a lead pipe, baseball bat, two-by-four, lamp, frying pan, hammer, sledgehammer. In the remainder of this chapter, if we refer to one such object, we are talking about any or all of them.

2. *Weapons that cut.* Most commonly a knife, razor, or broken bottle. What we tell you about defending against a knife is true of defending against any cutting weapon.

3. *Guns.* There are many different kinds, but your defense against them is the same.

None of these weapons alone can harm you. Surviving an armed attack depends upon fighting the attacker, not the weapon.

The Man with the Weapon

Because most American citizens do not carry weapons with them on the streets, criminals who do arm themselves feel a sense of great power and control carrying a gun, knife, or blunt object. Such an attacker is, without a doubt, the most cowardly of all. He is afraid of confronting someone with whom he is evenly matched. If he thought for one second that you were armed with the same weapon he has, he would want no part of attacking you. History bears this out. Whenever women have armed themselves, rapists go somewhere else.

In 1966 there was a surge in rapes in Orlando, Florida. The women said they were going to arm themselves. The newspaper and the police department advised against it, but since women were buying guns, the department offered a firearms safety course. Two thousand women showed up for the first one, and were sent home. Ultimately, as many as six thousand women were trained in how to safely use their newly purchased firearms. The result: the number of rapes and rape attempts dropped by 50 percent in the next year, and by 92 percent over the following two years. During those two years not a single woman actually shot a rapist. The mere possibility of an armed "victim" frightened the rapists away.

Any man who attacks you or threatens you with a weapon is doing so because he feels that the weapon gives him an unfair advantage. He thinks the weapon gives him control over you. But what he believes to be his advantage can become *your* advantage. His confidence that the weapon gives him power makes him completely unprepared for your challenge.

Defense against an armed assailant is, in large measure, about reaction time. How fast can you react and how quickly can the attacker react to you or to the situation? You can use the element of surprise to this end, as well as any other means you may have to confuse and slow him down, make him think and scare him back. He is not fearless. If he were, he wouldn't be picking on you and he wouldn't be hiding behind a weapon.

Isolating the Weapon

Have you ever held a gun, a crowbar, or knife, or other blunt object? The answer to the last two is almost certainly yes (if you've ever eaten steak or cut fresh bread or played softball), and it is doubtful that you feel threatened by the mere size and shape of these objects. As for a gun, if you have never held one, we advise that you do. Walk into a gun store with your training partner and ask to hold one or two or three different pistols. Hold one in your hand. Look at it. It is not a bomb. It is a tool, a potentially lethal one. But the key word is "potential."

There are many firearms safety courses for women. We highly recommend Paxton Quigley's (author of *Armed and Female*) classes as well as the National Rifle Association's Personal Safety courses. A gun—and any other weapon—is merely an extension of the will of the person holding it. Your aim is to fight the person, not the weapon.

Your immediate goal is not to disarm the attacker. If you focus all of your attention on the weapon, then you weaken your effectiveness. Rather, you isolate the weapon. What does that mean? Simple: move it enough so that it is not an immediate threat. A weapon can seriously hurt you only if it is aimed at you. Once the weapon is isolated, fight the person holding it. You may, in the process, disarm him, but that is not essential to survival. If you knock him unconscious, the weapon is no longer a threat (unless you try to handle it and do not know how to do so safely).

Isolating the weapon requires you to be proximate to the attacker. In fact, you have a much better chance against an attacker with a gun if he is one foot away rather than five feet away. From five feet away, he can shoot with little challenge. From one foot away, you can isolate the weapon. But we take this one step further. If you are attacked with a weapon and you retreat, you run a much greater risk of death or severe injury than if you attack. If you are shot and back away, the gunman can keep shooting. If you are shot and rush the gunman, you have a chance. It is the last thing he is expecting, and that surprise can enable you to isolate the weapon and disarm him. The same can be true with knives and other weapons.

Adrenaline, Calm, and Simplicity

There are many different ways to fight opponents with weapons. If you know anyone who is a martial artist, combat soldier, or police officer, you may have seen demonstrations of some. The problem with most of these techniques is that in order to work they must be mastered. That is because they require fine motor coordination, which is the first thing you lose when under great stress. Such skills can take years to master.

For this very reason, the techniques presented in this chapter are simple and do not require fine motor coordination. Thus, they can be learned in a very short period of time. Most of what you will learn in this chapter will be an extension of what you learned in previous chapters. Once you have isolated the weapon and reduced its threat, you will use the same hand strikes and arm strikes and kicks discussed in previous chapters.

This is not to diminish the potential danger of an armed attacker. Anytime you are threatened with a weapon, every fraction of a second becomes critical. You want to let your adrenaline pump you up, but you must also be thinking quickly and clearly. Energy and calm.

A Note About Practicing

In previous chapters we have suggested practicing techniques as we describe them with a friend. You probably cannot expect to learn them as completely in this manner as our students do when they have the opportunity to use what they learn against a practice attacker in full padding. Nevertheless, we believe that you can become skilled enough in them to make a difference. The techniques in this chapter, however, require much greater precision. If you miss a heel palm to the nose and catch the unarmed attacker's chin, you can still have an impact. But where weapons are concerned, you need to be more exact.

For this reason, we suggest that it is essential that you practice these techniques IN SLOW MOTION with a friend over and over. Remember, what your body learns in slow motion, it can recall and use at full speed.

Be sure to follow through on each movement. Slow motion does not mean half motion or stopping at the surface. Slow motion refers to speed only, not to the completeness of each movement. Make sure that you follow through on everything you do. If you follow through in slow motion now, you will follow through at full speed should you ever have to.

Be absolutely sure that you do everything in slow motion. Even at medium speed, your friend runs a very high risk of injury.

Also, make sure your friend knows and understands that you are going to follow through, so that she or he wears a groin cup and face mask and moves with your motion without resistance.

In Your Face

Just as we began our defense against unarmed assaults with those from a standing position, we begin the defense against armed assaults with those in which you are on your feet and the assailant is in clear view.

This scenario can begin a lot like the very first one in Chapter Four. The location can be almost anywhere—familiar or strange—though it is most likely an isolated place such as a deserted street, a building hallway, an underground parking garage. You are approached by a man, or you feel that you are about to be. You are uneasy. You trust your instincts and go into the freeze-walk stance, on the balls of your feet, knees bent, elbows together, arms up and waving in front of your face. Only this time the man approaching you has something in his hand. Watch the hands! The defense against a firearm starts differently from that against a knife or club.

A frontal assault can also come without warning. You could be charged with the weapon. If that is the case, then Step 1 of this technique is irrelevant. If you are charged, you charge also. Use your momentum against his and go directly to Step 2. But if it is not yet clear that you are going to be attacked, here is your response:

1. Assume the freeze-walk stance. At this point you may or may not be his target. There may be a chance that you can diffuse the situation, talk your way out of this without having to fight. As we discussed in Chapter Four, your stance and your demeanor are neither intimidated nor intimidating. You may make him uneasy and get him to back off. But you must be ready for the possibility that his actions will escalate—that he will suddenly attack or threaten you with the weapon. But whether he verbally threatens you or not, if you feel threatened you have a legal right to attack. Your chance of survival may depend upon acting as soon as you feel threatened, not

waiting until it is too late. Once you make this commitment, go all out. You may get bruised, cut, or even shot, but you are much less likely to be seriously injured or killed than if you go at him cautiously.

Once your eyes see a weapon and you determine that you must act to defend yourself, your arms and hands can adjust to its location and execute the following disarm if the assailant is coming toward you with a club or knife:

2. Rush toward him off-line. Rush means charge toward him with full commitment. Off-line means the following: imagine an invisible line between the weapon and its target—your head or body—and run around that invisible line.

3. Turn your hands sideways. The palms should be facing each other. These "ridge hands" and forearms are still out at a forty-five-degree angle.

4. Strike with both hands toward his wrist holding the weapon. The weapon in his hand is only as lethal as his hand can make it. You should chop all the way through with your intention.

The wrist is a relatively weak part of the arm, and so you can, in some cases, cause an attacker to drop the weapon. However, whether you think you may have disarmed him or not, keep fighting him. Don't reach to pick up the weapon. Keep attacking. If he reached down for the weapon—or anything else—find a target, his head or groin, and knee it. Knock him out and his weapon is of no use to him. Knock him at least into a daze and then you will have a clear opportunity to seize the weapon.

The follow-through will be the same for a charging club or knife as a hostage situation, so let's look at the differences now.

Hostage Situation in Your Face

If the assailant is facing you with a knife at your throat or points a gun in your face,

1. Stay calm; breathe. This may seem obvious, but believe us, when you are faced with this situation, it is easy to panic and

stop breathing. You need to be able to think and to act fast, and that requires oxygen in your brain and throughout your body.

2. **Compliance.** The first thing you want to do is let the assailant know that you are going to do whatever he says. He may tell you not to move, to freeze. It is all right to express fear. He expects you to be afraid. In fact, you can exaggerate your fear and seem more flustered than you are. At this point you want to find out what he wants so that, if possible, you can give it to him. Perhaps all he wants is money. No problem. Tell him where it is; tell him he can have it. But do not assume that he will be satisfied. Be prepared to defend yourself.

He may demand that you put your hands in the air. Whether he does or not, that is what you want to do. Put up both hands, but not way up, not over your head. What you want to do is position your hands slightly above the wrist of your assailant.

If the attacker has not instructed you, you might tell him that you are putting your hands up, so that he knows you are going to cooperate. As your hands slowly go up, get your feet in stance position (pelvis tucked, knees bent, feet apart, one foot slightly ahead of the other). Make sure that you are on the balls of your feet with your pelvis tucked and your knees bent. This is life or death. If any of these are not prepared, it could cost you your life.

3. Identify where the knife is—and in which direction it can be moved without cutting you. This will determine on which side you will strike his wrist.

If your assailant is holding a pistol to your face, identify which way you can strike the pistol without the discharge hitting someone you care about (like your friend standing next to you).

4. Calmly talk to him—as you slowly get your hands up in a "surrender" position. One hand should be close to his wrist holding the weapon; your other hand should be back.

5. If possible, before you make your move, try to get the attacker to think. You can slow his reflexes considerably by asking a question. Even something simple, such as, "Why are

Knife on the left

Strike to the left

Knife on the right

Strike to the right

you doing this?'' can confuse him and make it easier to disarm him. Saying something off the wall can have an even greater effect. "What's the frequency?'' "Where are the two thousand elephants?'' This may seem silly, but a question like that can throw an attacker, make him think, distract him. Pick your question now and use it all the time in practice. In the middle of a negotiation, you don't want to slow your reaction time by trying to think up a clever retort!

Once you ask, don't wait for an answer—spring into action with full commitment. We have mentioned commitment before, but in this case, it needs further emphasis. It is possible that you will be hit or cut or shot at. You cannot allow that to slow your defense. Remember that image of yourself as a child. That is what you are fighting to protect. If the gun goes off, it will make a loud, deafening blast, possibly very close to your ear. You are singular in your objective. You are going to survive, whatever it takes.

Strike his wrist

If you are facing a pistol, close your eyes like a blink, because when you strike the assailant's wrist, the pistol may or may not go off. If it does go off, the bullet should miss you (we use plastic guns that shoot plastic pellets in class), but the hot gases of the muzzle blast could blind you if your eyes are open.

6. Strike the wrist. If you hit the inside of his wrist hard enough, the blow can paralyze his hand and cause him to drop his weapon. However, don't depend on this. Do NOT try to grab his wrist. Grabbing is much slower than a strike, and when milliseconds count, it could mean the difference between life and death.

   The follow-through will be the same for each defense against an armed assailant, no matter which weapon or no matter which hand it's in.

Pin the weapon

Thigh to the groin

7. Pull down and hang on to the wrist. With both hands, quickly reach over his wrist and grab it with a thumbless grip. The chopping motion should flow easily into a strong, two-handed thumbless grip. We are assuming, of course, that he still has the weapon in his hand; it is important to assume this, because in the tunnel vision of a fight, you may not notice whether he is still armed and you must, for your own survival, assume that he is. The thumbless grip is simple. Grip with the four fingers like a hook (thumbs can easily be sprained if you try to use them as part of your grip).

8. Isolate the weapon in against your hip. Pull down hard on his wrist and bring it in against your hip. Done correctly, this move should aim the weapon away from or behind you.

   The power of this move comes from the pect-lat lock, which underscores the importance of keeping the elbows together. If your elbows are spread apart, you probably aren't going to have enough strength to pull the attacker's wrist in.

9. Thigh to the groin. At this point the attacker is completely focused on the weapon and his struggle to control it. The last thing he is expecting is a thigh to his groin . . .

10. Thigh to the nose. Take one step forward with the opposite foot and then use the same thigh that struck the groin and drive it into his head—which will likely have bent forward in reaction to your thigh to the groin. Throughout all of these moves, be sure to keep that weapon hand pinned to your hip!

11. Walk him to the ground. Allow the momentum of your thigh to his head to carry you forward. Step fast, moving him backward. He will likely be off-balance and will fall. Maintain your thumbless grip at his wrist, pinning it to your hip.

If he falls, let his weight carry you. If not, force him down with your weight. In either case, drop down, bending your knees next to him. Keep your back erect.

Thigh to the nose

Maintain your thumbless grip at his wrist, pinning it to your hip, then roll to your side.

12. Draw your legs in and kick the attacker's head with your top leg. As you bring your legs up and in, still gripping his wrist, you can hyperextend his arm—and even break it. This is what we call "Rope-A-Dope."

    Often, this alone will cause the weapon to fall. But do not look for it. Get those legs in and kick. Use side-thrust kicks and ax kicks until he is unconscious.

13. Pick up the weapon. The moment you feel able to do so without making yourself vulnerable to attack, grab the weapon, whatever it is. Pick it up carefully. If it is a knife, grab it by the handle—not by the blade. This may seem obvious, but in the throes of battle, your mind may be on automatic pilot. Former students have made this mistake and cut their hands needlessly. If it is a gun, do not put your finger on the trigger, and always point the muzzle in a safe

Walk him to the ground

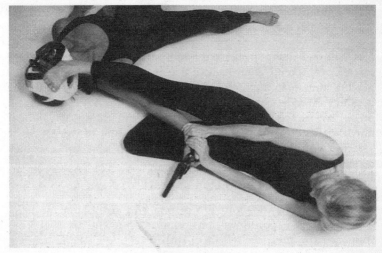

"Rope-a-Dope"

direction. In an adrenaline state, you could easily discharge it without realizing—and fire a bullet that could hit an innocent person in the vicinity. If the attacker lunges at you and you have the gun, it would not be unreasonable to use it. But remember, if you allow the external weapon to become the total focus of your attack, you become vulnerable. If you do not see the weapon at first, do not panic. Be sure to check around the assailant's hand and body, but do not spend too much time searching for it. It's far more important to get to safety.

14. Look, assess, and get help. As you do this, hold the weapon with both hands above your head.

   This reduces the chances of an accident harming you or an innocent bystander.

15. If you now have a weapon in your hand, especially a gun or a knife, be cautious. Do not rush at a stranger with the weapon. The stranger does not know that you just fought for your life; he may think you are an insane person attacking him. Keep your distance. Do not hold the weapon in a man-

ner that could be threatening—do not aim it in the direction of the person or hold it low, as if you are trying to conceal it.

If you feel that you can trust the person from whom you are asking help, keep your back erect as you slowly kneel, gently placing the weapon to the side of you, not pointing it in the person's direction or within his or her arm's reach. Stand up in protective stance, hands up, palms out, and calmly ask him or her to call 911. And use a nonthreatening tone of voice.

If you are trained in how to render pistols safe, you can tuck it behind you into your belt. We caution against tucking an unsheathed blade into your belt, since, unlike a pistol, a blade is "always loaded"!

If you feel uneasy about the person you are asking for help, don't set the weapon down, but point it up in the air away from your face (or anyone else's face) with your finger off the trigger.

Practice these entire moves, shouting NO with each strike.

CHARGING CLUB OR KNIFE

- Freeze-walk stance.

- Rush toward him off-line.

- Hands are up at a forty-five-degree angle turned sideways—"ridge hands."

- Strike the wrist holding the weapon (follow-through).

HOSTAGE IN YOUR FACE

- Freeze-walk stance.

- Comply with the initial request unless it endangers you further.

- Determine neutralizing direction of your strike.

- Ask your stupid question (if facing a gun, close your eyes).

- Strike the wrist holding the weapon.

THE FOLLOW-THROUGH IS THE SAME:

- Use a thumbless grip to bring the weapon down to your hip; keep it pinned there.

- Thigh to the groin, then take an extra step.

- Thigh to the head.

- Walk him to the ground; you go forward, he goes backward. Keep his wrist pinned to your hip.

- Roll to your side and draw your legs in.

- Finish him off with ground kicks.

- Pick up the weapon.

- Look, assess, and get help.

- Gently place the weapon next to you on the ground.

- Rise in stance, palms out.

- Ask someone to please call 911.

Again, ideally you can practice this on a friend, in slow motion, but realistically that can be dangerous for the subject. In our workshops we often give the "attacker" a false arm so that his real one does not get broken. As for the weapons, we use replicas in our workshops—plastic knives, toy guns, foam or rubber bats or clubs. The more they look and feel real, the better.

However you practice and whatever you use, the most important thing is to practice in slow motion to reinforce good habits.

Standing Hostage—One Hand Pinned (Hook Technique)

There is one slight variation of the standing defense against an armed attacker from the front. In some cases, an attacker can hold a knife to your throat while holding one of your arms, either at your side or across your back in an arm lock.

1. Stay calm; breathe.

2. Identify where the knife is—and in which direction it can be moved without cutting you. Because one hand is pinned, you won't choose which hand strikes him, but rather, from which side you will HOOK his wrist, and in which direction you will push the blade with your free hand.

3. Calmly talk to him—as you slowly get your free hand up in your "surrender" position.

4. Ask your nonsense question.

5. Hook the wrist. With your free hand, quickly reach over and around his wrist and grab it with a thumbless grip.

6. Pull it down toward your hip. With the strength of your whole body, pull down on his wrist. At this point your other hand

Hook the wrist

may be able to break free and help grab his wrist with a thumbless grip, as you . . . do the follow-through.

Practice the sequence:

- Stay calm and breathe.

- Determine the safe direction for your hook.

- Calmly get into a surrender position.

- Ask your stupid question. Close your eyes if you're going against a pistol.

- Hook.

- Follow through.

From Behind Your Back

Using your ears, eyes, and intuition can help you avoid a sneak attack. But not always. In armed assaults against women, less than half were rear assaults, cowards with weapons jumping out of nowhere. There are two basic kinds of attacks:

1. Weapon in the back or back of the neck or head

2. Weapon at or around the throat

As with all other attacks—armed or otherwise—you need to be ready for a threatened attack (one in which the assailant wields the weapon and makes a demand) as well as a sudden attack. In the case of the latter—when you are suddenly attacked—you must explode instantly into action (beginning with Step 4). In the case of the former, you need to read the situation. What does he want? If he wants money or other property, give it to him. If he says he wants sex, then you might be able to wait until you are in a better position—one in which you can see the weapon—in order to attack and disarm him.

At some point you may realize that you must act, that he is going to use his weapon or that he is going to rape you. Here is how.

Gun or Knife in Your Back or at the Back of Your Head

For the opening steps, treat this exactly as you would if you were a hostage with the assailant in front of you.

1. Stay calm and breathe.

2. Determine the angle of attack and the safe way to neutralize the threat.

3. Comply as long as it doesn't endanger you further. Get into your surrender position, arms spread way back (even with your shoulders) and adjusting to the level of the weapon. Place one foot slightly ahead of the other. Being on the balls of your feet with knees bent and pelvis tucked is absolutely critical here.

4. Ask your stupid question.

5. Spin around to chop his wrist. In one swift and powerful movement, let your hips and upper legs propel you into a 180-degree pivot on the balls of your feet. Keep your hands up and flex your arms. They will collide with the hand holding the weapon.

You may knock the weapon out of his hand. You may not. Don't think about that. Fight as though he is still holding it. This sequence flows easily into the next move.

6. Isolate the wrist and weapon. Quickly target the wrist holding the weapon. With two hands, using a thumbless grip, bring it to your hip.

Done correctly, this move pins his wrist to your hip and the weapon is aimed away from or behind you the same as before.

Remember, the power of this move comes from the pect-lat lock, so be sure to keep your elbows close to your body.

The follow-through is, again, exactly as before!

Practice this sequence over and over.

Arms back

Pivot

Chop his wrist

- Freeze-walk stance. Imagine the weapon in your back or at the back of your head.

- Tell him you're going to put your hands up in the air.

- Put your hands up, slowly, raising them to the same level as his weapon.

- Ask your stupid question to distract him, then—

- Spin, which causes you to—

- Strike at his wrist.

- Thumbless grip to his wrist; isolate the weapon hard against your hip.

- Follow through.

Practice it in slow motion three times spinning to the right, three times spinning to the left.

As we said above, ideally you can practice this on your training partner, in slow motion, but realistically that can be dangerous for your partner. When you are the practice attacker, don't stick your finger into the trigger guard, and keep your thumb on the same side as your palm. We realize this is not the correct way to hold a pistol, but since the disarm is designed for self-defense, its goal is to break the trigger finger, dislocate the thumb, and break the wrist. However, bear in mind that the fight is not over until you have gotten help and gotten away.

What if at some point during the fight you lose control of the hand holding the weapon? What if you lose sight of where the weapon is? The answer is simple. Fight the attacker. The sooner you knock him out, the less chance there is that he can recover and harm you. Yes, the idea of fighting an armed attacker and not knowing if you are about to be shot, stabbed, or clubbed is frightening, but your priority is clear. You kick and kick. Take care of business and you can survive.

This is by far and away the most dangerous disarm. The average criminal's reaction time to pull a trigger is .7 seconds. My reaction time is .2 seconds. When I asked twenty members of a major metropolitan SWAT team to try their disarming technique, from this position, I shot sixteen in the head. When they tried our techniques, I was able to shoot only one in the head. After I perfected his techniques, even he could move on me without my being able to hit. I cannot recommend enough that you take this full-contact class from an authorized Model Mugging instructor. It's better to make your mistakes in class against plastic guns and bullets than on the street.

Standing Hostage Position: Knife (or other weapon) at Throat from Behind

This is certainly one of the most frightening positions to find yourself in—a blade at your throat. It calls for an immediate and alert reaction. Assume the freeze-walk stance on the balls of your feet, knees bent for balance and pelvis tucked.

1. Stay calm; breathe.

2. Identify where the knife is—and in which direction it can be moved without cutting you and where his wrist with the knife is.

   If he is right-handed and behind you with a hand around your neck holding a knife, his wrist would be at your right shoulder. Therefore, your hands come up in front of your right shoulder. If he is left-handed, your hands come up in front of your left shoulder. For the sake of clarity, we will describe the move for a right-handed attacker. When you practice, do so this way as well as from the opposite side (simply change right to left and left to right and practice the same moves).

3. Calmly talk to him as you slowly bring both hands up in a "surrender," targeting his wrist.

4. Bring both arms in tight for a pect-lat lock. Feel the flexing of the pectoral muscles.

5. Ask your stupid question to make him think.

6. Both hands turn toward him in a thumbless grip on his wrist. Reach quickly with both hands and grasp the wrist holding the weapon.

Try to be as precise as possible so that if it is a knife, you do not accidentally grab the blade. If you do, you can still disarm the attacker, but when it is over, you will probably need stitches on your hand. We break this move down into its component parts, but when you do this move, the thumb-less grip and the next step must be performed in rapid succession. Be sure to maintain the peck-lat lock; that is where your power comes from for your next move.

7. Pin the wrist and the weapon to your upper chest above your breasts. This is VERY IMPORTANT! Keep the weapon pinned for ALL of the following moves. By doing so, you are pitting your entire body weight, strength, and momentum against his wrist and elbow. Again, it is more efficient to pull the blade all the way to your hip, but this causes your partner's hand to slide over your breast. Therefore, for personal boundary issues during training, we keep the pull to the upper chest.

8. Butt-strike and pull down on the wrist, keeping it pinned to your chest. The idea is not to push the weapon away from your throat. You pull down and in against your chest. A good butt strike and pull-down—keeping the wrist pinned—will actually rotate the blade away from your throat.

Because the attacker's pressure is in and not up, you are not struggling against his muscle. Down and in. He is not in a position to resist. Nor is he prepared for your next move:

The follow-through is exactly like the rear-choke defense, but we will review it here.

9. Left foot steps forward to one o'clock. It is a simple movement. Keeping the wrist pinned that holds the weapon, you step forward at a slight angle which extends the attacker's arm.

10. With your left foot again, step to the left of him. He will be on your right side now. The key is to keep his wrist pinned to your chest as you step, which will twist his arm.

You should land facing the opposite direction of where you started and standing to the left of the attacker. This move, done

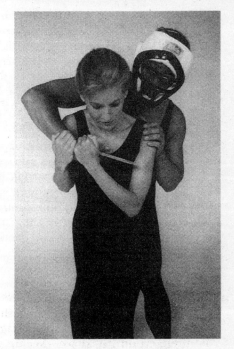

Pin the weapon to your chest

correctly—quickly and with a firm grip on the assailant's wrist—can potentially break his arm.

If possible, practice this move repeatedly. Imagine the arm with the knife or blunt object around your neck. Keep still but maintain your balance on the balls of your feet, keep the knees bent, bring your hands up as if surrendering but really finding his wrist. Then:

- Ask him a question to distract him.

- Thumbless grip with both hands on his wrist.

- Pin it to your chest as you—

- Butt-strike.

- Step way out in front of you to the one o'clock position with your left foot.

- With your left foot again, step to the left of him (he will be on your right), keeping his wrist firmly planted to your chest.

Obviously, this is a move you must practice with some degree of caution. You don't want to break anyone's arm. In our workshops we use a false arm—any padded pole about two feet long will do.

If you have a left-handed assailant, this same move will throw the assailant to the ground as you break his wrist and elbow. Unless you and your training partner have judo or aikido experience, we don't suggest that you practice this maneuver with each other except in ultraslow motion, without the partner falling.

Of course, if you have broken the assailant's arm, it isn't likely he will still be holding a weapon, but you cannot assume that.

11. Right thigh to his groin. Since your left foot and head are to the side of him, you are in a perfect position to drive your right knee through his groin. By keeping your head to the side of him, you won't get head-butted when he lurches forward quickly after the thigh to the groin.

    Make sure that as you do this, you do not lose your grip on the wrist with the weapon. The rest of this technique you already know.

12. Extra step with left foot.

13. Right thigh to the head.

14. Walk him to the ground. Keep his wrist pinned to your chest with both of your hands.

15. Get your legs in and kick his head.

16. Pick up the weapon.

17. Look, assess, yell NO! and get help.

Practice this entire sequence—as best and safely as you can. Do it three times as if the knife is in his right hand, three times as if the knife is in his left hand, in ultraslow motion.

On the Ground

If you can do the ground-release techniques from the last chapter, you can modify them and defend against an armed assailant, starting on your back or on your stomach. If you have not yet mastered those techniques, you should do so before attempting to modify them as described below.

Basically, there are three ways in which we modify ground releases to combat armed attackers: 1) neutralizing the threat of the weapon, 2) controlling the weapon during the release, and 3) controlling the weapon while knocking the assailant out.

On Your Back— Club or Knife Striking Downward

As always, your immediate response will depend upon the imminence of harm. If the assailant is already clubbing, stabbing, or shooting, you act. If not, you wait for your opportunity.

If he is sitting on your chest and attacking:

1. Using your pect-lat lock, bring both arms up to strike the descending wrist and the weapon-holding hand.

2. Almost simultaneously, bring up your right knee.

3. Thrust the assailant off you.

4. Thumbless grip to slam his wrist against the ground.

5. Thigh to the groin.

6. While pinning his weapon hand to the ground, pivot your hip so you can—

7. Kick him repeatedly in the nose.

8. Keep kicking until he is unconscious.

9. Carefully pick up the weapon.

10. Look, assess, yell NO! and get help.

Practice this technique as best you can with a partner in slow motion.

Weapon striking downward

Strike his wrist

Thumbless grip

Hostage Pin, on Your Back, His Knife at Your Throat or Gun in Your Face

There are two variations, and each is similar to the standing hostage: knife at the throat technique we teach. The primary difference is, of course, that in this case, you are on your back. As with the standing-hostage release, the first three moves are the same; then the moves vary depending on whether one or both hands are free.

1. Comply and negotiate.

2. Determine the line of attack.

3. Slowly lift the leg opposite the weapon hand and plant the foot. (You must thrust your hip in the same direction you are knocking his hand.)

4. Pect-lat lock as you fake surrender by getting your hands up. Note how similar this is to the defense against an armed assailant in a standing position, only this time you are on your back. One hand should be close to his wrist with the weapon, your other hand back. If it's a gun, close your eyes.

5. Ask your confusing question.

6. Strike his wrist.

7. Using both hands, make a thumbless grab on the wrist.

8. Pull down, simultaneously thrusting him with the hip. Be aware of the knife or muzzle direction as you move.

The follow-through is the same as before.

Hostage Pin, on Your Back, Knife at Your Throat or Gun in Your Face— with Your Striking Hand Pinned

Hook technique: to be used if an attacker is sitting on you or lying between your legs and holding a knife to your throat while pinning one of your hands with his free hand.

1. Comply and negotiate.

2. Determine the angle of attack.

3. Slowly lift the leg opposite the weapon hand and plant the foot. (You must thrust your hip in the same direction you are knocking his hand.)

4. Pect-lat lock as you fake surrender by getting your hands up. Note how similar this is to the defense against an armed assailant in a standing position, only this time you are on your back. Because one hand is pinned, you won't choose which hand strikes him, but rather, from which side you will HOOK his wrist, and in which direction you will push the blade.

5. Ask your confusing question.

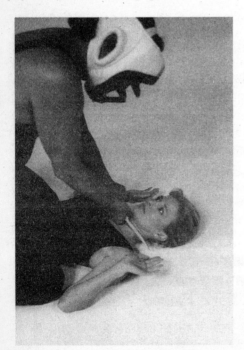

**Weapon at throat,
one hand pinned**

Hook his wrist   **Pull wrist to ground**

6. Hook the wrist. Quickly reach over his wrist and grab it with a thumbless grip. Your pect-lat lock is critical here.

7. Pull his wrist down to the ground. At this point, your other hand may be able to break free and help grab his wrist with a thumbless grip, as you—

8. Thrust with your hip, tossing him off. This thrust will help send the knife away from your throat. Remember, your left foot planted tosses him to your right; right foot planted sends him to your left.

NOTE: Moves 6, 7, and 8 are done almost simultaneously. The follow-through is the same as before.

Practice this in ultraslow motion. When done correctly, this can break his wrist and slam his head into the ground.

On Your Stomach with Attacker Between Your Legs, Knife Under Your Throat

This is probably the most dangerous knife release. Fortunately, it is also a rare position for anyone to attempt a rape with—since it would require tremendous coordination to keep a knife at your throat while carrying out a rape. Because our philosophy is to OVERtrain our students, we have developed a technique for this situation.

In this position, you are on your stomach and he is on your back, his legs between yours with all of his weight on your back and a knife beneath your throat.

This may seem an inescapable position—but it is not.

1. Stay calm; breathe; think.

2. Identify which of his hands holds the weapon. That is the direction in which you will throw him. If the knife is in his right hand, throw him right; if it's in his left hand, throw him left.

Plant foot, thumbless grip

Toss him off

3. Locate the wrist. See exactly where it is in relation to your neck and your hand.

4. Calmly talk to him—as you slowly get your hands and feet in position. Bring up the leg and foot on the side OPPOSITE the direction you are going to throw him (e.g., if you are going to throw him right, bring up your left leg and plant the left foot). At the same time, slide both hands up toward the wrist holding the weapon. Because he is on your back, it is possible for you to make these moves without his noticing.

5. Ask your nonsense question to distract him.

6. Reach quickly; thumbless grip on the wrist.

7. Pin his wrist to your shoulder. This move is similar to one used against the standing rear position. Keep the wrist that holds the knife pinned against your chest with your pect-lat lock as you—

8. Thrust back with your hip, tossing him off. Remember, your left foot planted tosses him to your right; your right foot planted sends him to your left.

Roll and kick

9. Quickly roll in the opposite direction. If you tossed him right, roll back left; if you tossed him left, roll back right. Keep his wrist pinned.

10. Get your legs in and kick his head. Maintain your grip on the wrist with the weapon, extending the attacker's arm as you move away.

The follow-through is the same.

Once again, this is designed to be dangerous to the attacker by breaking the wrist and elbow. *Go ultraslow*, because your body can generate tremendous force in simple rolls against your partner's vulnerable joints.

When Clubbed, Stabbed, or Shot

This is a very scary thought, but it might happen before you realize that you're being attacked. Everyone needs to develop the body reactions that keep one fighting—it's not over!

A single gunshot wound is fatal only 10 percent of the time. Take the guy out and you stand a good chance of surviving. If you give up, he may shoot you again. Each time he shoots, your chances to live decrease.

So we practice our drills in which the practice assailant clubs gently with a foam club, stabs gently with a rubber knife, and shoots the fighter with a plastic bullet from a plastic gun. The first time is psychologically and physically jarring. The fighter then takes the assailant out. Our students are trained to react to injury in *one* new way only—fight back!

When one of our instructors was trying to talk his way out of a physical confrontation with an assailant in front of him, another clubbed him over the head from behind. Fortunately, this instructor's wife had taken Model Mugging and was able to take that assailant out.

Another student hit her head on the concrete when being knocked to the ground. She defended herself successfully and then fell unconscious.

Do not allow yourself to be discouraged. We are asking you to absorb a lot of material, to learn a great deal—more, perhaps, than you might feel capable of. Do not expect yourself to get it all right away. Allow your mind and body to become accustomed to these fighting skills, to process them between practice sessions. You'll get it. Don't rush yourself. Every skill you acquire is one you did not possess yesterday.

We spend an entire weekend teaching the material in this chapter alone with a ratio of 1 professional instructor to 8 students. Of course, it will take you and your partner longer, but you can learn this. Your life depends on it.

We do an exercise on Saturday night in which we ask the students to call a very close friend and explain they need help completing an exercise for a self-defense class.

The topic of the discussion is, "If I were going to die tomorrow, this is what I want to say to you tonight." Again, use the format of 1) appreciations, 2) worries and fears, each being turned into a problem with a solution, and 3) hopes and aspirations.

More than anything else, this exercise will get you in touch with your desire to live.

You may also decide to rearrange your priorities. When contemplating death, ordinary things become significant. You will take less for granted. You will choose to live fully in the moment.

Although this is done as an exercise, we can't really know if we will live tomorrow. I [Matt] recently drove to a photographic modeling assignment (hardly a high-risk assignment) in the pouring rain. A car swerved in front of me. I swerved to avoid crashing into it and my four-wheel-drive Land Cruiser spun out. With the help of evasive driving classes, I was able to control my spin through four lanes of traffic without hitting anyone and was congratulating myself until I went over a forty-foot embankment. My four-by-four flipped and landed on its roof. If I hadn't installed a four-posted roll cage inside to protect my children, I would have been killed. I was knocked unconscious for forty-five minutes, and later discovered that someone had looted the contents of my vehicle.

The lessons I learned were: 1) Being prepared saved my life. 2) Live each day fully, because we never know when our lives might end.

When my oldest son was only six, he was climbing to the top branches of a tree. I said, "Be careful." He replied, "You know, Dad, everything you do in life, you risk your life." I said, "Be careful as you enjoy climbing the tree!"

By facing death in class, we yearn to live.

The fear of death will not paralyze us; if faced with an armed assailant, we know how and can act.

Action beats reaction so we can live.

So let's live each day fully, passionately, and with purpose!

CHAPTER EIGHT

Fighting Multiple Assailants

COWARDS WHO ATTACK women will use any advantage they can, and that includes outnumbering the victim. Incidents of multiple-assailant attacks are, unfortunately, on the rise—especially with the increase in street-gang activity—though such assaults still represent the minority.

The idea of fighting two or three men at once may seem hopeless, but it is not. In fact, graduates of our basic self-defense course (designed to fend off a single assailant) have, in several cases, successfully defended themselves against multiple attackers.

One graduate was coming out of a store with her cousin—who was eight months pregnant—when they were surrounded by four assailants. The graduate asked them to let her pregnant cousin go and promised them the time of their lives if they did (remember, it's okay to lie to a rapist!). The men agreed, and when her cousin was gone our heroine was grabbed from behind. She elbowed the man in the nose, dropping him instantly. A second attacker grabbed her in a bear hug. She hammer-fisted him in the groin, dropping him as well. She turned to the other two and in a strong voice asked if they wanted more of the same. They retreated—and as she was leaving, she noticed that they had to carry the guy she'd hammer-fisted to the getaway car. On another occasion, our heroine was subsequently confronted by a local gang of teenaged thugs who were trying to assault her daughters. Again she knew what to do: she identified the leader and heel-palmed him in the nose. Once he was down, his gang exposed themselves as the wimps they really were and ran.

Understanding the gang psychology of these cowards and building on techniques you've already learned, you will be able to develop the potential to fend off more than one man at a time.

Neanderthal Man in Modern Society

As with all self-defense techniques, the defense against multiple assailants is informed by our understanding of the predator/prey dynamics.

Although in many respects we have evolved quite far from our primitive ancestors, when it comes to attack and defense, very little has changed. Men who attack women are predators; their targets are their prey. Using numbers as a predatorial advantage goes back millions of years (in fact, it is one significant reason that humans even exist today). In the evolutionary process, humans became the dominant species largely because of our ability to control and manipulate things with our thumbs, and because of our ability to communicate plans with one another. This enabled a team of primitive humans to take on a huge woolly mammoth or a cave bear. This same advantage can be—and is—exploited against other humans—as when more than one man attacks a woman.

But being outnumbered and being outsized are not the primary problems with fighting against a herd or pack of predators. Interestingly, the greatest challenge of fighting the herd is to avoid becoming confused. When a deer (think multiple pointed, pitchforklike antlers and four lightning-fast, sharp, hard hooves—not Bambi), which could easily defeat a single wolf, is attacked by a pack of wolves, the deer lashes out ineffectively at many wolves or tries to run and then is brought down and eaten by the pack.

Therein lies our challenge: how to fight two or more attackers at once without diffusing your defense and becoming ineffectual.

Fortunately, your advanced mind has the potential to enable you to prevail over your attackers and their primal instincts—especially if you . . .

Build On What You Know

In defending yourself against multiple assailants:

1. Entering the mind of the assailant(s) is even more critical.

2. Action still beats reaction; at best you will be only one step ahead of your assailants, and therefore, a preemptive strike now becomes almost mandatory.

3. You must instantly heighten your energy level to its maximum because you may have to hit multiple attackers repeatedly.

4. The shout is even more important as a psychological weapon since it can add to the demoralization of the rest of the attackers.

5. Dropping to the ground no longer is advantageous, because you can open yourself up to kicks in the head from behind. Mobility becomes one of your most important assets.

6. More than ever, you cannot afford to give up, because if you surrender, each assailant will try to outdo the damage caused by the others.

7. The physical fighting techniques are almost the same; what differs is the openings.

8. Positioning is key; the strategy is a little like that found in a football playbook.

Avoidance Is Still The Best Defense

Growing up in that orphanage in Japan, I [Matt] often had to fight multiple attackers. Those early experiences taught me profound lessons about protecting myself from the pack.

Avoid Being Alone

Early on in the orphanage, I discovered that I was far more likely to be attacked when I was by myself than when I was with one of my friends. Soon my cribmate, Carlos, and I began to travel everywhere we could together. We were still attacked, but together we were a much better fighting force than either of us could ever hope to be individually. To this day, that still represents a sound principle I try to follow whenever I have to go to a place I suspect might present danger. Police departments know this—that is why you will almost never see a single officer patrolling a dangerous neighborhood. Police teams further rely on their radio so they can call for backup the minute they become aware of danger. Let's face it: even the so-called Lone Ranger had a partner who saved his bacon all the time!

Watch Your Back

Often, the greatest threat to your safety is not the enemy you see—it's the enemy you don't see. When Carlos and I were together in the orphanage, whenever we suspected the presence of a potential attack, we immediately checked out our rear. We'd go back-to-back, unless we were up against a wall, in which case I took the left and he took the right, since I am left-handed and he was right-handed.

Make a Heightened State of Awareness Your Norm

The perils of my early years gave me the gift of extreme alertness. It became second nature, and I overlooked nothing in my surroundings. Intensified peripheral vision is a wonderful thing—and not just in terms of self-defense. It also helps me to notice and appreciate the beauty that is around me, and it is a thing worth learning.

Two Keys to a Heightened Awareness

If you don't see an attack coming, you are at a tremendous disadvantage and will lose the fight before realizing it has started. No one can detect every threat at every moment, but you can greatly increase your perceptive abilities by maximizing your peripheral vision and utilizing reflection.

- Maximizing peripheral vision

The human eye can see almost ninety degrees to the right or left. Thus, if you have the use of both eyes, you have almost 180-degree vision. See for yourself:

Looking straight ahead, reach your hands out to your sides with the fingers up. Wiggle them and see how the motion detectors in your eyes pick them up.

Now keep your arms outstretched and look straight ahead, raising your hands to see how high you can perceive; then lower your hands to see how low you can perceive.

Look toward the ground and notice how much you can still see of what's in front of you.

Now turn your head without twisting your torso and note how little you need to turn to see what is directly behind you, using your peripheral vision.

Remember, you need not make eye contact with an assailant to identify him and act to defend yourself.

- Utilizing reflection

Nor do you have to have the assailant in your line of vision at all in order to observe him. Walk down the street and observe the people around you—actually count them—using not only your straight-on and peripheral vision but also the reflective surfaces of car windows, store windows, and mirrors. It is remarkable how much you can see in an urban environment without turning your head.

You can, and should, practice this: simply find two people willing to be your training partners. On various streets, at various angles, have them try to sneak up on you—and use peripheral vision and reflection to thwart them.

First Lines of Defense
Against Multiple Assailants

- As always, the best defense is AVOIDANCE

  With a heightened sense of awareness, you should be better able to identify a potentially alarming situation, and your response should always—without question—be: MOVE, if at all possible!

  Also, by making a move away from the threat, you can determine if, in fact, it is a threat. If the danger you perceive is real, and your potential assailant moves to block your escape or chase you, then that is your cue to turn your movement into an attack.

- Positioning

  One of the key principles of fighting multiple opponents is the diffusion of their advantage by drawing them into a strategically weakened position. A perfect example of this occurred during the Russo-Japanese War. The powerful Russian navy sailed halfway around the world and was defeated by one of the most simple, classic maneuvers of the Japanese ships crossing the T. Here is how it worked. The Russian ships were in a convoy toward Japan.

X X X X X X X X

But as they were approaching, before they had a chance to fan out, the Japanese ships confronted them in a line perpendicular to their approach like this:

X → X → X → X → X → X → X → X→ ←O
←O
←O
←O
←O
←O
←O

All but one of the Russian gun turrets wound up pointed at each other's backs, while all of the Japanese cannons were turned for broadsides.

For our purposes, if three or four opponents are lined up one behind the other in relation to you, only one opponent presents an immediate threat. In a line, you face only one assailant at a time.

Of course, the attackers don't want to attack in this position and thus will try to reposition themselves, but chances are they have not rehearsed such a move and will likely be indecisive. Their hesitancy is their weakness. Their hesitancy is your opportunity to attack while they are off guard.

- Selection

    Finally, the fact that herds almost always have a leader means that if you can break the morale of the leader, you can break the morale of his followers and get them to flee. From anthropology we learn that the early battles in human history were fought by gangs. In those battles, a particular side would usually suffer casualties of about 10 percent—unless the morale of one side broke, in which case its members would try to run and could suffer up to 90 percent casualties.

    Though there are no foolproof techniques for identifying the leader, he is often the one doing the talking. You can also tell by watching the eyes. Followers will often look at their leader—far more than he will look at them.

Difficult to Practice, but Worth the Effort

As with our other techniques, practice is key to preparation. However, the techniques for defending against multiple assailants will be the most difficult to practice safely.

This is the case for two reasons. To begin with, defending against multiple assailants requires more precision than defending against a single assailant. Even in the movies, some of the most accomplished martial artists of our time have to carefully choreograph the multiple-attack sequences—and have the luxury of multiple takes, which a woman fighting for her life does not.

Practicing these moves will also require two partners, preferably people who are also interested in learning this technique. Hopefully you haven't thoroughly trashed your training partner and the two of you are still friends! As always, partner practice requires mutual respect and mutual cooperation. The purpose of the training for the defender is not just to practice techniques, but to rehearse victory.

This rehearsal must, for safety reasons, be done step by step in slow motion—to ensure preciseness—with the defender counting out each step. As the defender, you must always make the first move. Have each of your stand-in attackers take his first move while you take your second move—to simulate being only one step ahead of your opponents.

Do the best you can with practice. What you cannot safely practice with companions in this step-by-step manner, practice in your head until it becomes second nature.

STANDING DEFENSE

You have already learned how to defend against an unarmed or armed assailant from a standing position (to review, see Chapter Four, page 54, and Chapter Seven, page 138). The techniques you have learned—and, hopefully, practiced and perfected—are the same techniques you will utilize here, with two significant alterations:

1. A flanking maneuver which can enable you to fight the assailants one at a time.

2. With multiple assailants, ground fighting is far more risky, since you can be kicked in the head from behind. Therefore, as long as there are two conscious assailants, you should avoid going to the ground.

There are a variety of scenarios against multiple assailants from a standing position, and, as in previous chapters, we will begin with the most simple and straightforward kind of attack and work our way into the more complex. You will discover that the defense varies only slightly among these different situations.

Two Attackers from the Front

In this scenario, you are approached by two men, both visible. They make a threatening move toward you. You don't wait for them to strike first. Their threat to your safety is your cue for action.

1. Scan your surroundings. While keeping track of them with your peripheral vision, quickly scan behind you to see if there are any other attackers.

2. Distract the attackers. Make a confusing comment or ask a stupid question. If you have been able to identify which of the assailants is the leader, direct the comment or question to him.

3. Flanking maneuver. Without pause, launch into a flanking maneuver with hands up in protective stance. Move to the right or left so that one attacker is directly between you and the other attacker.

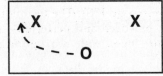 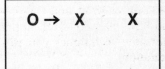

4. Face the attackers from the flank. From this angle you are facing only one. At this point these cowards might back off. If so, you back away from them, cautiously, not letting down your guard. If they come toward you or try to flank you then—

5. Attack. Without hesitation, you must charge immediately and with 100 percent energy. Repeatedly heel-palm, thigh-to-the-groin, thigh-to-the-head.

   If the second attacker tries to flank in one direction, flank in the opposite direction.

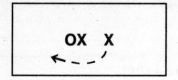 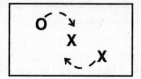

Continue using heel palms and knees to the groin until the first attacker is down.

Remember: DO NOT drop to the ground and kick. Doing so can place you in a vulnerable position with more than one attacker.

Instead, immediately launch into the second attacker while his morale is weak and his mental state is indecisive. Do not give him a chance to recover or his fear might turn to anger against you.

If at this point either or both attackers try to flee, do not chase them.

Otherwise, continue heel palms, thighs to the groin, and thighs to the head until both attackers either run or are down.

6. Look, assess, and yell NO! at each knocked-out assailant, being careful never to walk between them. Go around! Then get help. As you leave the area, be extra cautious and watch out for additional partners who might be lurking.

A black belt in karate I [Matt] knew was attacked by two assailants. He was Japanese and very polite, so he used only minimal force to deter the two attackers. While he was listening to their pleas to let them go, he was stabbed in the back by a third assailant and killed.

Practice these moves, especially the flanking maneuver, with awareness at all times.

Two Attackers from the Rear

In this scenario, you are approached from behind. Using reflection and/or peripheral vision, you see two assailants.

1. Scan your surroundings. Continue looking over your shoulder and keep track of them with your peripheral vision.

2. Distract the attackers. Make a confusing comment or ask a stupid question.

3. Spin around, hands up, and flank. Immediately pivot 270 degrees, spinning yourself around into a flanking maneuver so that you face only one attacker.

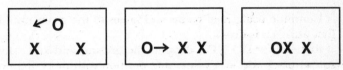

4. Attack. With 100 percent energy, charge the attacker directly in front of you, repeatedly heel-palm, thigh-to-the-groin, thigh-to the-head.

   If the second attacker tries to flank in one direction, flank in the opposite direction.

   Continue using heel palms and thighs to the groin until the first attacker is down. Then do the same to the second attacker.

5. Look, assess, yell NO! and get help—being extra cautious and watching out for additional assailants.

   Practice these moves. Again, pay special attention to the flanking maneuver.

Two Attackers: One in Front, One Approaching from the Rear

In this scenario, you start in a more vulnerable position: between the two assailants. Yet your response is almost identical to your response against two assailants from behind.

1. Scan your surroundings. Using reflection and peripheral vision, keep track of both assailants.

2. Distract the attackers. The moment you sense danger, make a confusing comment or ask a stupid question.

3. Spin around, flank. In this situation, the assailants are expecting one of three things: that you will try to run, that you

will freeze up in terror, or that you will try to stand up to the attacker facing you. What they are not expecting is for you to turn and attack the assailant behind you—and so that is what you do: a sudden pivot, about 135 degrees, and then a flanking maneuver.

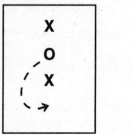 

4. Attack. At the same time you flank, charge and, with 100 percent energy, repeatedly heel-palm, thigh-to-the-groin, thigh-to-the-head. Do not stop or hesitate until both assailants are either unconscious or have fled the scene.

5. Look, assess, yell NO! and get help.

Practice these moves, especially the flanking maneuver.

Two Attackers: One in Front, One Holding You from the Rear

There are a variety of different holds an assailant can use to try to restrain you while his partner attacks. The response to these holds is virtually the same. You quickly assess; then you attack.

1. Scan the situation. In this scenario, you have likely been attacked by surprise and it is too late for the freeze-walk stance. However, using reflection and peripheral vision, you can still make quick note of both assailants and their locations and determine whether or not there are others.

2. Distract the attackers. When the attacker facing you is within one step of you, make your confusing comment or ask a stupid question.

3. Bring your arms up and kick. Get them as close to a "ready position" as the hold will allow. Simultaneously, kick the assailant in front of you, using either a straight-legged soccer kick with your instep or a thigh to his groin, depending on how close you are to him.

   Follow that with a thigh in his face when he bends over.

4. Release from the hold. Use the skills in Chapter Five:

   - Butt strike, hip shift and hammer fist.

   - Elbow to the nose.

   - Heel palm to the nose.

   - Thigh to the groin.

   - Thigh to the nose.

Arms up and kick

5. Spin around, flank. Immediately launch into a flanking maneuver, moving around the assailant who had faced you, and attack him with heel palm and thighs to the groin and head.

6. Look, assess, yell NO! and get help.

Two Attackers: One on Either Side, Both with Holds on You

As in the previous scenario, there are a variety of different holds that dual assailants can use to try to restrain you while they attack. And again, the response to these holds is virtually the same. You quickly assess; then you attack.

1. Scan the situation. Again, this is a scenario in which you have likely been attacked by surprise and it is too late for the freeze-walk stance. However, using reflection and peripheral vision, you can still make quick note of the number of assailants and their locations.

2. Distract the attackers. Make your confusing comment or ask a stupid question.

3. Pect-lat lock. Lock one arm into a pect-lat lock and relax the opposite arm. This will allow you to pivot toward the assailant who is holding your locked arm.

4. Pivot and attack. Pivot toward the attacker who holds your pect-lat locked arm and thigh him in the groin. When he bends over, thigh him in the face.

5. Repeat the move, other side. Immediately relax the arm you've now freed, and pect-lat-lock the other. Pivot into the other assailant and thigh him in the groin; when he bends over, thigh him in the head.

6. Break away and continue to flank. When both arms are free, position yourself so that one assailant is always between you and the other and attack the assailant in front of you.

7. Continue to attack. Repeat your attack into whichever assailant poses the greatest threat, until both are down.

8. Look, assess, yell NO! and get help.

GROUND DEFENSE

Although we teach students to stay on their feet when fighting multiple assailants, obviously there is no guarantee you will be able to—or that the battle won't begin on the ground. You might have already guessed that much of what we teach our students to prepare for a ground defense against multiple assailants is a combination of our regular ground-fighting techniques and our techniques for fighting multiple assailants.

If for any reason you find yourself on the ground against more than one assailant, don't try to stand up. Trying to rise will make you even more vulnerable to attack. Although standing mobility is preferable against multiple assailants, you can still defend yourself from the ground.

You're on the Ground: Two Attackers Standing in Front

1. Scan the situation. Try to determine whether there are any more attackers and, if so, where they are.

2. Distract the attackers. Ask a stupid or off-the-wall question.

3. Flanking maneuver. Because you are on the ground, the flanking maneuver becomes a "rolling log." Bring your arms and elbows into a pect-lat lock and roll into a flanking position.

Surprise and commitment are the essential keys to the success of this move. It is likely that the attackers will be wondering what the hell you're doing, and that wondering will further distract them from their objective.

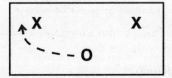 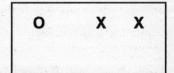

4. Kick the closest assailant. In the side-thrust-kick position, launch a series of kicks into the knees and groin of the assailant closest to you at that moment.

NOTE: If you practice this move, you must go ultraslow or you can seriously injure your partners. In our classes we no longer allow kicks to the knees of our "model muggers," because even with all the armor we wear, it is impossible to ensure that their knees won't be blown out by students.

5. Attack the other assailant. When the assailant closest to you falls, maneuver on the ground until you're in position to kick the other assailant. Continue until both assailants appear to be unconscious. Then carefully and cautiously get up.

6. Look, assess, yell NO! and get help.

On the Ground, Faceup: One Assailant Above Your Head Holding Your Arms, the Other Holding Your Feet/Ankles

This is a challenging position to escape from, since your arms and legs—the very weapons we have taught you to use—are constrained. But it is not possible for one person to hold your feet and your knees simultaneously—and therein lies your escape.

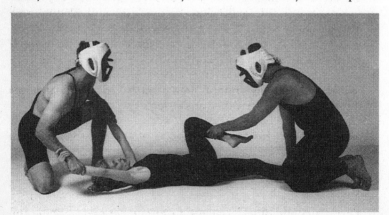

Windup for side-thrust-kick to his thumb

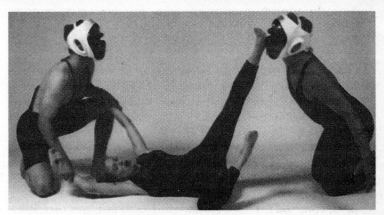

Side-thrust-kick his face

1. Scan the situation. As always, try to determine whether there are any more attackers and where they are.

2. Distract the attackers. Ask a stupid or off-the-wall question.

3. Countergrab the assailant holding your arms.

4. To break the man's hold at your feet: twist your hips until you're on one side and bring the top knee up with the same intensity as a windup for a side-thrust kick. It's your thigh muscles against his thumb, so you should break his grip. If you don't break his grip, don't worry—continue to attack.

5. Side-thrust-kick his thumb. Immediately side-thrust-kick his thumb holding your other ankle/leg.

6. Side-thrust-kick his face. Either one of the previous two maneuvers will likely bring his face into range for you to shift your hips and side-thrust-kick him in the face with your other foot.

7. Thrust-kick the other assailant. Continue countergrabbing the man holding your wrists/arms as you spin completely around,

Spin and kick

rotating your hips into position to side- or front-thrust-kick the second assailant's face.

8. Flank the assailants. Maneuver into a flanking position to launch kicks into the first assailant. Continue kicking until both assailants are down or flee.

9. Look, assess, yell NO! and get help.

On the Ground, Facedown: One Assailant Above Your Head Holding Your Arms, the Other Holding Your Feet/Ankles

This defense varies only slightly from the previous one. Since you are facedown rather than faceup, your hip rotation is different.

1. Scan the situation. This will be difficult since you are facing down, but using peripheral vision and paying attention to whether the assailants in your view are making eye contact with anyone else, you can make an assessment as to whether there are more than two attackers.

2. Distract the attackers. Ask a stupid or off-the-wall question.

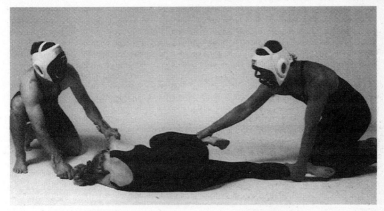

Windup for side-thrust-kick to his thumb

3. Countergrab the assailant holding your arms throughout this move. Twist your hips until you're on one side and bring the top knee up with the same intensity as a windup for a side-thrust kick. It's your thigh muscles against his thumb, so you should break free of his grip. Even if you don't break his grip, don't worry—continue to attack.

4. Side-thrust-kick his thumb. Immediately side-thrust-kick his thumb holding your other ankle/leg.

5. Side-thrust-kick his face. Either one of the previous two maneuvers will likely bring his face into range for you to quickly roll onto your back, continuing until you're on your other side, and side- or front-thrust-kick him in the face with your other foot.

6. Thrust-kick the other assailant. Continue countergrabbing the man holding your wrists/arms. Spin 180 degrees, so that your hips are in position for a side- or front-thrust kick into the second assailant's face.

7. Flank the assailants. Maneuver into a flanking position to launch kicks into the first assailant. Continue kicking until both assailants are down or flee.

8. Look, assess, yell NO! and get help.

Spin and kick

On the Ground, Faceup: One Assailant Above Your Head Holding Your Arms, the Other Sitting or Lying on You

1. Scan the situation. As always, try to determine whether there are any more attackers and, if so, where they are.

2. Distract the attackers. Ask a stupid or off-the-wall question.

3. Countergrab and release from the pin. This move, from this position, is very similar to the escape from a faceup position against a single assailant—with the addition of the countergrab. First, countergrab the wrists of assailant #1 above your head. Then bring your arms into a pect-lat lock. At the same time, bring one knee up and thrust assailant #2 off your stomach or from between your legs, using the rape-release sequence from Chapter Six.

4. Attack assailant #2. Immediately attack the assailant you just threw off. Use front-thrust kicks to his face or, if he is still in close to you, thigh him in his groin.

5. Attack assailant #1. Spin, rotate your hips, and roll into a position to front- or side-thrust-kick the assailant holding your arms. If he is in too close for you to use thrust kicks, use ax kicks until he lets go of your arms.

6. Flank the assailants. Maneuver into a flanking position to launch kicks into assailant #1. Continue kicking until both assailants are down or flee.

7. Look, assess, yell NO! and get help.

On the Ground, Facedown: One Assailant Above Your Head Holding Your Arms, the Other Sitting or Lying on You

1. Scan the situation. Again, this will be difficult since you are facing down, but using peripheral vision and the eye movements of the assailants, it is possible to assess whether there are more than two attackers.

2. Distract the attackers. Ask a stupid or off-the-wall question.

3. Countergrab and release from the pin. Countergrab the wrists of assailant #1 (the one holding your arms). Use the "stomach pin" release sequence from Chapter Six—bring your knee up like a lizard, plant your foot, and thrust with your hip—to knock assailant #2 off your back or from between your legs.

4. Attack assailant #2. Use the momentum to roll onto your back and immediately start ax-kicking him in his groin—alternating feet—and rotating your buttocks to ax-kick him in the head.

5. Attack assailant #1. Continue countergrabbing his wrists and rotating your hips. Roll into position for front- or side-thrust kicks to the assailant holding your arms. (Because assailant #1 is still grabbing your wrists, there is a limit to how far you can twist, but you should be able to position yourself to kick him.) Then start kicking.

6. Flank both assailants. Maneuver into a flanking position to launch kicks into assailant #1. Continue kicking until both assailants are down or until both flee.

7. Look, assess, yell NO! and get help. Leave the area, being extra cautious and watching out for additional partners who might be lurking.

Lying on Your Side on the Ground: Mugger Sandwich

This is almost identical to the standing situation where one assailant has grabbed you from behind and one is in front—except that this time you and the assailants are on the ground, with one assailant facing you, the other one behind you, both of them grabbing some part of you.

1. Scan the situation. As always, try to determine whether there are any more attackers and, if so, where they are.

2. Distract the attackers. Ask a stupid or off-the-wall question.

3. Frontal assault against assailant #1. Use your proximity to him to launch an all-out assault of thighs to his groin, heel palms to his nose. Shift your hips in order to kick him in the head.

4. Takedown release against assailant #2. Though you're both already on the ground, you can still use the takedown release from Chapter Five to free yourself from the attacker holding you from the rear:

   - Butt strike to the groin.
   - Hip shift.
   - Hammer fist to the groin.
   - Elbow to the nose.
   - Turn to face him.
   - Heel palm to the nose.
   - Thigh to the groin.

5. Roll yourself over him so that he is between you and assailant #1 . . .
   Then launch an all-out kicking assault against him. If assailant #1 tries to come over #2 in order to get at you, he'll make a nice target for a kick to his head. If he doesn't try to come over his partner to get you—

6. Flank the assailants. Maneuver into a flanking position to launch kicks into assailant #1. Continue kicking until both assailants are down or flee.

7. Look, assess, yell NO! and get help.

Mental Preparation for Multiple Assailants

It's unlikely that any of us face attacks by multiple assailants every day. However, almost all of us have multiple problems every day, and it's a good bet that we feel others have ganged up on us earlier in our lives in some way or another.

The net result is that psychologically we carry memories of "inner muggers" as well as multiple "current external muggers."

WRITING EXERCISE

Write down an early experience when you felt "ganged up on." How did you react? With your current mental and physical tools, how would you react differently?

Try using this format: 1) Establish priorities. Which problems are more serious? Which problems need to be dealt with right away? 2) Flank; use a little energy to distance yourself from one problem in order to 3) Focus on the main problem. How do you focus on the main problem? By turning worries and fears into problems with solutions with hopes and aspirations for a better future. Now do the same with the second problem. Lo and behold, what we learned for warfare can be used in everyday times of peace.

A Final Word: Practice and Confidence

That's it. If you've read this far, then you've read all of our "Model Mugging" self-defense techniques. With practice, you can make them your weapons of survival. In our classes we require another weekend with one professional instructor per eight students to teach just the material in this one chapter. You will have to practice longer on the techniques described in this chapter with capable and willing partners to make yourself truly prepared for an attack by multiple assailants.

Yet just knowing these techniques has proved to be enough for some of our former students. We've already told stories about several graduates of our classes who—despite taking only the level-one class, which dealt with the defense against a single, unarmed assailant—managed to successfully defend themselves against more than one attacker.

Several years ago we began an experimental class specifically for students over sixty. One of our students in that class, a sixty-nine-year-old man, was subsequently approached by two men with knives. He faked a heart attack, and as the first assailant came within range, he side-thrust-kicked him in the knee. There was a loud snap, and the assailant fell to the ground screaming in pain and dropped his knife. The other assailant fled.

This same man was later approached by two men with knives in a subway station. This time he acted compliant at first and explained that he needed to stand up to get his wallet out of his pocket, then stood up, kneed one assailant in the groin, double-clapped the eardrums (which we no longer teach, even though it can be effective), and kneed the assailant in the face, dropping him. The accomplice fled.

None of the students mentioned above had taken the multiple-assailant class. But they had confidence in themselves and were able to allow their own survival instincts to take over. They adapted to the situation and utilized what they had learned.

They did their best—which is all that anyone can ever do.

And that was enough.

CHAPTER NINE

Expect The Unexpected: Legal Aspects of Self-Defense

IN THE MOVIES, when a crime victim becomes victor—successfully defending herself against an attacker usually with excessive bloodythirsty force—the audience cheers. The heroine buries herself in the arms of her lover/husband/child and the credits roll. She doesn't worry about the police, about possible arrest or a lawsuit. In real life, however, those possibilities, outrageous as they may seem, are very real.

Women aren't expected to defend themselves—and one of the occupational hazards of police work is the necessity to make split-second decisions, to make assumptions. Criminals, obviously, are not trustworthy and will often lie, if given the opportunity, to try to incriminate a victim. Furthermore, we live in a litigious culture. Frivolous lawsuits are rampant. Not long ago, a burglar, trying to break into a school at night, fell through a sky window, sued the school district for negligence, and won more than one million dollars.

Take nothing for granted.

In this chapter we will first address the ways to ensure that your defense is always within the law. Then we will discuss what to do immediately after the fight, including how to deal with police so that you don't get hurt and so that you don't mistakenly incriminate yourself. We will also suggest ways to deal with the possible aftermath of your successful defense to protect against potential criminal charges or a nuisance lawsuit.

Of course, the advice we present is not meant to be exhaustive, and since the circumstances of each assault situation will vary, the general rules we will explain may not apply to your situation. Everyone should, of course, consult his or her personal attorney if legal action is threatened. Nonetheless, the following discussion should give you a general overview of the legal principles involved in self-defense.

If you are appalled at the thought of possibly having to mount a legal defense after you have just mounted a physical defense, you probably should be. It is incredibly unfair—but it is reality. Chances are you won't be prosecuted or sued—but why take chances? Be prepared.

Know Your Rights—and Wrongs— of Self-Defense

Most citizens are aware of their right (in fact, it is a right shared by most people living anywhere in the world) to defend themselves from attack. This right extends all the way to kill in self-defense, if that is necessary to stop their attack.

But self-defense, is not an unconditional right. You may not, for example, kill someone simply because that person attempted to harm you. If the attacker is already unconscious—and you know that he is—you may not legally continue to punch or kick him.

The conditions of self-defense do not mean that you are required to memorize the penal code. But you do need to fully understand the principles behind them. You may use only the force necessary to defend yourself from physical harm and no more. Put another way: you are allowed to use enough self-defense to ensure your own survival. Of course, under the conditions of a street fight, you cannot be expected to know the moment your attacker is unconscious or to know his intentions. Rather, your justification comes from how you—and how any reasonable person in your situation—would perceive the situation.

If someone attacks you, you have reasonable cause to fear for your life and to fight until you are sure that you are safe. If the attacker says he's sorry in the middle of the fight, you DO NOT have to let him go—because he could be lying—and if you stop fighting, he might take advantage of you. If your attacker appears to be seriously injured, you DO NOT have to stop defending yourself. If he cries and says his arm or leg is broken and he needs help, you are not in a position to trust him. He may be lying. He may be trying to lure you back into a compromising position. Keep kicking him until he is unconscious. Ted Bundy, an infamous serial killer, used to wear a cast on his arm and ask women for help; then he'd use the cast to knock the woman out, rendering her defenseless.

Generally, you should have the legal right to keep kicking until the attacker is unconscious, to keep going until he goes limp. Only then can you be certain that the attacker poses no further danger to you.

You have a right to survival, and once an attacker breaches human trust by coming after you, your survival depends, not upon trusting him, but upon believing and fearing that your life is in danger.

If someone tells you he's going to harm you and he moves within his striking distance apparently ready to attack, you have reason to fear for your safety and may therefore legally act pre-emptively to defend yourself. If you are in a defensive posture—as is the freeze-walk stance, if your language is not combative—you are telling him to back off; you are saying you do not want any trouble—then you cannot be accused of mutual combat, of provoking the fight.

If you disarm your attacker in the course of a fight, you may use his weapon against him, provided that he is still an imminent threat to you.

No Street Justice

Once your attacker is lying prone, not moving, you may not stab or shoot him. Nor, for that matter, can you kick him in that position, much as you may believe he deserves it and more.

You may not fight out of vengeance. That is never legal. You may not attack someone because he or she made you angry. If someone angers you and you strike, you have committed a crime. By the same token, once it becomes clear to you that your attacker is unconscious, the fight is legally over.

Put another way: you may not do more than is reasonably necessary to eliminate the threat. You cannot legally continue your counterattack in order to seek justice. You may feel that our justice system will not sufficiently punish your attacker and that you yourself want to do it. You may find yourself wanting to kill or maim him so that he never attacks another woman—but you do not have the legal right to do that. It is not your prerogative to mete out justice.

Your goal, once your attacker is unconscious, should be the same goal that enabled you to fend him off: the drive for self-preservation. To that end, get yourself to safety, however you can best achieve that, given the situation.

The Good Guys Aren't Supposed to Win— but the Truth Will Emerge

Actually, the first part of that is a myth—one our students have helped to dispel—but it is a myth that many law enforcement officers continue to believe.

For that reason, police officers arriving on a crime scene who see a woman standing over someone (especially if she is holding his weapon) can easily perceive the woman as a hooker who has just rolled a john.

Be prepared for this situation.

Some police suspicions of you can be mitigated if you are the one who called them or instructed a witness to do so. But even then, at the moment the police arrive, it is their professional obligation to take absolute control of the situation.

Our warnings here are not meant to give you second thoughts about self-defense or the police. Far from it. If you are in the right—if you are defending yourself from a legitimately perceived harm—then the right and legal thing to do is whatever it reasonably takes to neutralize the attacker.

Perceptions are a gray area in the law. So are motives. How

can anyone prove what is in someone else's mind? But remember: when you are under pressure, you will do what comes naturally. Concealing things is, for most people, an act that requires thought and at least some preparation. If you are interrogated at the scene of the fight, you very likely will tell the truth as you know it at that moment. You will say exactly what is in your mind. If you tell the police something like, "I sure as hell taught that fucker a lesson!" or, "I hope I killed him!" that statement could be viewed as a confession that you went further than was necessary to protect yourself.

If you fight out of self-love and preservation, you are more likely to blurt out something like, "He attacked me! He tried to rape me. I fought him off."

Always comply with the demands of the police officers. If they tell you to freeze, do so. Do not express anger or outrage. The officers are there to help. They are not in as big a hurry to find out what has happened as you are to tell them. Their priority is to take control of the situation, for the safety of everyone.

If you have a weapon, let your hand go limp to show you have no intention of turning it on them. When they tell you to drop the weapon, bend down and gently lay it on the ground.

The officers are in a high-adrenaline state. They probably had a high-speed run with sirens blaring. They don't know what to expect. Everything you say should be simple, a minimum of words, and easy to understand because they, too, are under tremendous stress.

The officers may be responding to a 911 call placed by a friend of the attacker who might have implicated you as the criminal. This is especially possible if you have been the victim of an attempted date rape. Police officers are used to such disputes, and their approach is simple: they believe neither side. So don't argue. Some cops roll from felony to felony. Their job makes them somewhat cynical.

The first thing you should say to the officers is:

- "Thank God you're here."

This statement can be effective on several levels. To begin with, the words "thank you" are not something the officers are used to hearing from criminals. Also, the word "God" can be reassuring, whether or not the officers are religious or spiritual. Call it cultural persuasion.

The second thing you should say to the officers is:

- "I'm [first name] and I'm a(an) [occupation]."

Using your first name only gives the officers another cue that you are their friend, that you are on the same side. Also, and perhaps more important, if you say your last name, you are exposing yourself to your attacker and any of his friends who might be in the area. Your last name can easily lead someone to your door, either to stalk you or to intimidate you so that you don't prosecute. When the officer asks for your last name, say you have identification but you don't want to give your name to the attacker. This again identifies you as the "good person."

Telling the officers your profession is a good way to make it clear that you are NOT a prostitute or other criminal. It is essential you make that clear. For example, if you are a massage therapist, just say "therapist." If you are a dancer, make it clear that you are a "ballerina."

The third thing you should say is:

- "This man attacked me."

It is a simple statement that lets the officers know that you need their help. But don't try to tell them any details. Under stress, you are likely to experience short-term memory loss. You might not remember certain details that you will remember later. If you make conflicting statements, you will find yourself vulnerable to cross-examination if criminal charges are filed against your attacker or against you. The less you say about the incident, the less likely you are to contradict yourself. This is the exact advice given to police officers involved in shootings or other uses of force.

The fourth thing you should say is:

- "I need a doctor."

This statement is important for three reasons. To begin with, you could in fact be injured, perhaps seriously, and you may not be aware of it. One former student broke her wrist hitting an attacker and had no idea that there was anything wrong with her until two days later. Others have sustained broken thumbs, arms, ribs, and shoulders without knowing it until much later.

Second, this statement again reminds the officers that you are someone who needs them. Their presence may be saving your life.

Finally, once you've requested a doctor, your statements are no longer held to the same standard as they otherwise might be. If there are conflicts between what you say now and later, your lawyer can point out that you were in a state of mental and physical trauma.

The fifth thing you should say is:

- "Should I talk to an attorney?"

Notice, we do not suggest the statement, "I want to speak with my attorney ..." That suggests a familiarity with the process—and therefore, the possibility of guilt.

To this question, the officers should say, "Yes." If they say, "No," they have committed a dereliction of their duty. They are trained to advise you to seek legal counsel. In fact, police officers are told that if ever they are involved in a use of force or firearm, they should not make any statements until their lawyer is present.

Once the officers tell you that yes, you should contact your attorney, do not make any further statements until your attorney is present. So much can result from what you say under this hyperadrenaline state that you can regret later.

Review the above statements:

- "Thank God you're here."
- "I'm [first name] and I'm a(an) [occupation]."
- "This man attacked me."
- "I need a doctor."
- "Should I talk to an attorney?"

Practice them, in sequence, until they become automatic. Remember, in an adrenaline state, you will do and say what you have conditioned yourself to. This will prepare you for even the worst-case scenario.

The Worst-Case Scenario

The likelihood of this happening is slim, but the possibility exists, and being overtrained is better than being undertrained. In the worst-case scenario, you have just defended yourself against an attacker, and then the police arrive and treat you like a criminal. It won't seem fair, but if you resist, even a little, you may force the officers to hurt you. Put another way, if the police are at all suspicious of you, they will search and cuff you. They will do it the easy way or the hard way, depending upon how you react. Being arrested as a felon when you have done nothing wrong is horrible. But you can live through it.

Although each department has different procedures, this is what you might be told by a well-trained officer who is pointing a loaded pistol at you:

- POLICE!

- STOP!

- PUT THE WEAPON DOWN!

- STEP AWAY FROM THE WEAPON!

- DON'T LOOK AT ME!

- SLOWLY TURN AROUND!

- HANDS UP . . . HIGHER!

- ON YOUR KNEES!

- FACE DOWN!

- HANDS OUT TO YOUR SIDES!

- PALMS UP!

- CROSS YOUR ANKLES!

- LIFT THEM UP!

And if you say anything, you may likely be told: "SHUT UP!"

An officer might then kneel on your crossed ankles, forcing them to your back. This will hurt. It's supposed to—it's called "Pain-Compliance."

You will be frisked carefully over virtually your entire body. You might then have your breasts, groin, and anal area tapped with a pen to check for any concealed weapons.

All of the above can be extremely infuriating and humiliating. But none of those words are physically injurious in the long term.

If, however, you resist, verbally or physically, you run the risk of being forcefully taken down to the pavement and speed-cuffed—which will likely result in the handcuffs being agonizingly tight.

In this situation you want to let the officer know, verbally and physically, that you intend to comply. You also want to tell him that you think you need to see a doctor or get to the hospital.

I [Matt] have taught defensive tactics and weapons familiarization to about three thousand gang-suppression and SWAT officers. An officer who treats you like this is being a professional. All he knows is that you have been dangerous enough to render some bigger guy unconscious and probably bloody. At first sight, you may have been holding a weapon. It was your attacker's, but the police don't know that!

Remember, though, that this is the worst-case scenario.

Almost all of the officers who have responded to our female students defeating their assailants have been positive and helpful.

Our police truly are the thin blue shield that keeps the criminals at bay. Respect the fact that they need to protect themselves in order to keep doing their job.

Your Right to Flee

If, as is more likely to be the case, there are no witnesses and no police arrive on the scene, you have the legal right to leave the scene of the attack to get to safety.

If you remain there, the assailant can regain consciousness and he can harm you. Even if you have disarmed him and are aiming his gun at him, you are far from safe. Criminals practice disarming police officers—it is a favorite pastime while in jail.

You are not legally obliged to get your assailant help unless you are absolutely sure that your own safety has been achieved.

When you leave the scene, call one of two places.

If you feel that you are in grave mortal danger—if, for example, you believe your assailant knows where you live or work— call the police.

If you are not immediately in danger, call your attorney, then follow his or her advice on how to go about reporting the incident. If you do end up at the police station, it is preferable to do so in the company of your attorney. Police stations are full of criminals. They are not a good place for any person to be alone.

Criminal Rights and Wrongs

Although it is always a possibility, it is unlikely you'll be arrested after defending yourself. However, the person against whom you've just defended yourself can—and might—file criminal charges against you. Having just lost a fight to a woman, he may seek revenge, and some perverse honor—or he may do it in the hope of avoiding his own prosecution.

He may also be filing criminal charges as a precursor to a civil suit, especially if he is an acquaintance of yours. If you have assets or liability insurance, there are bound to be people who will jump at the opportunity to sue.

Most criminals have lawyers.

You should, too.

The Best Defense

Don't wait until something happens to get a lawyer. If our worst-case scenario should ever happen to you, you don't want to find yourself thumbing through the yellow pages for a lawyer when you're in a police station or a jail cell.

You want to have already established a relationship with an attorney you know and trust, and have his or her emergency telephone number with you at all times.

Find a good lawyer now, someone you like, someone you trust, someone on the right side of the law. If you pick the best criminal defense lawyer, the district attorney may assume you are a criminal (since criminals are the ones who keep those hotshot defense lawyers in business).

The best defense attorneys for innocent citizens usually are former D.A.s who are now in private practice. For one thing, they generally have a good relationship with the D.A.'s office. Former D.A.s know the law from being a prosecutor, and they are more than likely senior to the prosecutor assigned to your case.

We suggest calling your local district attorney's office and asking for the names of former D.A.s who've gone into private practice.

Better yet, find a lawyer known in the community for defending police officers.

Expert Witnesses

The strongest witness for your defense is a well-informed and legally versed YOU. Becoming well informed and legally versed has already begun with this chapter. We highly recommend, for further reading on this subject, *In the Gravest Extreme* by Massad Ayoob and *Armed and Female* by Paxton Quigley (although they deal specifically with armed defense, the same principles apply in an unarmed defense). Although there are no guarantees or certainties in matters of law, if you ever have to appear in court to justify using self-defense, these books along with our book can give you a lot of legal ammunition.

The authors can also back you up as expert witnesses if need be. True, this can potentially be expensive—flying in Massad Ayoob or Paxton Quigley. But the mere fact of having these names on your list of expert witnesses may get the opposing lawyers to think twice. Many district attorneys are career-minded. They want to succeed and get promoted, and thus, they need a good win/loss ratio. They don't like to lose.

Massad Ayoob is one of the most respected police trainers in the world and is also the most prolific writer on the subject. He does not testify on behalf of criminals—only citizens who've defended themselves against criminals, and unjustly accused police officers. He won't take a case unless he has investigated it first and believes his client to be in the right. And he has such an impressive record of influencing acquittals in these kinds of cases that no D.A. in his right mind is going to want to go up against him.

Paxton Quigly puts the same kind of fear into overzealous prosecutors. She has appeared on *60 Minutes* and numerous talk shows and in magazines, and is widely recognized as a spokesperson for a woman's right to arm and defend herself. We have worked with Paxton, and I [Matt] even gave her a few firearms lessons when she was researching her book. She believes very strongly in our approach and will back up any woman prosecuted for using our techniques to defend herself.

So far, of more than four hundred women who've used our psychological and physical defense techniques to defend themselves, none have been prosecuted.

As for civil cases, once criminal charges are dropped, the likelihood of anyone winning a civil case is greatly diminished. Lawyers in such cases usually work on a contingency—they get paid only if they win—and if they see those same expert witnesses listed, contingency lawyers are less likely to want the case.

So far, of all our former students who have successfully defended themselves, none have been sued, and only one was threatened with a lawsuit. She had defended herself against an attempted date rape and, in the process, had broken the assailant's jaw. He threatened a civil suit—probably to frighten her about reporting his crime—but she called his bluff and his suit never materialized.

Points to Remember

Some of what you have read in this chapter may seem like common sense. Some of it may seem disturbing, even shocking. If you are not a lawyer, it may seem like a lot to learn. But it need not be. Here are the main ideas to keep in mind. You can only legally fight if:

1. You are in fear for your life.

2. You reasonably believe your assailant has the capability of harming you.

3. Your assailant has demonstrated intent to harm you.

4. The danger of grave bodily harm is imminent. You do not, however, have to wait for your attacker to hit you. Imminent jeopardy means that you have reasonable cause to feel threatened, and that is justification to strike first. This can be a simple matter. For example, you have asked him to back off and he refuses; as you take a step backward, he advances toward you in a threatening manner.

5. You may legally keep hitting until he stops moving and appears to be unable to harm you. If you have any doubt, you can keep hitting or kicking. If he pleads with you to stop, you do not have to. Pleading can be a trick.

6. If police officers arrive, tell them, "Thank God you're here," followed by your first name and occupation. Tell them you need a doctor and ask if they think you should call a lawyer. After the police say yes, you should contact a lawyer, say no more. Only answer further questions under your attorney's instructions.

7. If the police do not arrive and there are no witnesses, do one of two things:

   a) If you are in imminent danger, call the police.
   b) If you are not in danger, call your lawyer.

8. Have a lawyer before you need one.

And above all, never worry about the legal aspects of self-defense while you are defending yourself. Only afterward, when you are safe, should you be concerned.

A proverb from the Old West is still true. "It is better to be tried by twelve than carried by six."

WRITING EXERCISE

Again, you learn by doing, so write down your reactions to this chapter to help you sort it out.

Then take action.

- Role-play the felony arrest with your training partner (forget the handcuffs; we're not into bondage!).

- Find a good lawyer.

- Read Massad Ayoob's book *In the Gravest Extreme.*

- Read Paxton Quigley's book *Armed and Female.*

- Rather than just seeing the police as the ones who pull you over for speeding, attend a police-crime-prevention community meeting and get to know police officers for their real job, "to protect and to serve"!

- If your community has a Civilian Ride-Along program, spend a night with an officer on patrol. Then you'll really appreciate our blue knights.

CHAPTER TEN

Believe in Your Power

WE THOUGHT A great deal about what to leave you with in this final chapter. In our classes, during the final group discussion before our graduation ceremony, we cover a number of issues, many of which are worth mentioning here. We focus primarily on day-to-day living—problems and solutions of a nonviolent nature—since the vast majority of our students are able to avoid ever having to use their newly acquired survival skills for an actual physical confrontation.

We begin, however, with a discussion about coping in the aftermath if you ever do have to physically defend yourself.

Heal Yourself

Whatever the outcome, if you ever have to use physical force to defend yourself, you are likely to experience trauma. Even when you win the fight, even if you have only minor physical injuries, you will probably have extensive emotional bruises.

Seek and get psychological counseling immediately. Don't be ashamed of your fear, anger, or even guilt. You may THINK that you're supposed to feel wonderful after successfully defending yourself, but that may not be the reality. It probably won't be.

Police officers involved in justifiable shootings are immediately given therapy. What's good enough for them ought to be good enough for you—especially when you consider this statistic: twice as many criminals are killed justifiably by citizens as by cops.

You may, after successfully defending yourself, feel guilty for hurting the assailant—especially if he is someone you know—even though you understand that you had to hurt him in order to protect yourself. Good people all have one thing in common: they don't want to hurt others. In many cases, we feel that how "good" we are is dependent on not hurting anyone. If that sounds like you, then you will need support. You will need someone to help you realize in your heart that what you did was right and that you can regret that it happened (regret what you were forced to do) while at the same time knowing that you are not at fault and that had you had another option, you would have taken it.

Some of you may have friends and family who will provide emotional support for you should you ever have to defend yourself, but there are no guarantees. The experiences of our students have taught us that reactions of friends and family vary wildly.

A fifty-two-year-old grandmother and former student of ours stuck her neck out and successfully defended a woman who was being assaulted in a parking lot. Most of her friends asked her why she did it and told her she shouldn't have, that she was foolish. The responses of the people in her life were so negative that she started to question herself. Only after she had spoken to Model Mugging instructors was she confident that she had done a noble and heroic thing.

You can be a loving, caring person and a potential killer. That you could hurt an attacker does not make you a mean person. In fact, if you hurt an attacker in order to preserve life—your or someone else's—you are the antithesis of a mean person. You are a warrior preserving life.

An Evolved Warrior Preserves Life

The goal of self-defense is, of course, never to have to use it. The paradox is that the more you know how to defend yourself and have confidence in your physical power to defeat an attacker, the less chance there is that you will ever have to use it. But the impact of knowing these fighting techniques and being able to tap into the mother-with-child adrenaline state can have a profound and lasting effect.

Self-defense is much more than fighting skills or a heightened awareness of safety and danger. It is a mental, emotional, even spiritual transformation—from victim (or the fear of victimhood) to evolved warrior.

Through the techniques and exercises in this book, we are confident that you can make that transformation.

The concept of an evolved, peaceful warrior comes from the literature of our good friend Dan Millman. He was my [Matt's] gymnastics coach when I first went to Stanford, and I've been blessed to train him and his family in my martial arts. He continues to be a valued mentor to my spiritual growth. His most famous book series, the Way of the Peaceful Warrior, has already inspired millions and we highly recommend it to you.

The true purpose of an evolved warrior is to preserve life.

Sometimes that preservation involves harming another, but the evolved warrior does so only when it is absolutely necessary.

Not when someone upsets her.

When an evolved warrior is called a name, she ignores it. When she is cut off on the freeway, she lets it go. If the situation is not life-threatening, it isn't worth fighting over.

I [Matt] have tried to live this philosophy in my life—and it has paid off:

Several years ago, while working as a professional bodyguard, I was hired to protect a Japanese client. We were in an après-ski bar in the Rockies and six guys started making anti-Japanese slurs. Now, believe me, if this had happened when I was younger, I probably would have fought. In a seventh-grade history class, a kid called me Jap. I took him out right there. I also took out two of his friends and knocked over five innocent people sitting at their desks—and was suspended from school.

Now I have the power not only to fight but to suppress any urge. So instead of attacking those bigots, I got up from my table (leaving my client sputtering), walked to the bar, and ordered Japanese beers for their table. I sat back down and watched the waitress bring them six beers. The waitress pointed to me, so I held up my bottle and hollered, "Hey, we Japs know how to do some things right!" The men laughed. One of them came over and apologized. He turned out to be an off-duty deputy sheriff. Had I challenged them, there might have been a fight. Had there been a fight, the deputy might have reached for his weapon—in which case I would have done the same (having trained thousands of police officers, I know that I can draw much faster than the average cop). I would have head-shot him and anyone else who went for a weapon. For what? A stupid racial slur. Leaving the bar, my client fumed: "I thought I was going to get to see what I pay you a thousand a day for . . ." I replied, "You just did." He never hired me again, but I knew I had done the right thing.

An evolved warrior is someone who has the ability to do great bodily harm to someone else but won't fight unless it is absolutely necessary. An evolved warrior will use any means available to avoid a fight. An evolved warrior will use physical force only to preserve life.

A Lifelong Commitment

We sincerely hope that when you finish this book you will not simply put it aside and forget about it. Rather, we hope that you will use these pages as an ongoing resource that you will refer to periodically.

Do the breathing and joint rotation warm-ups we recommend in Chapter Three. Beginning each day in this fashion will wake up your body and mind faster than coffee or tea, and it's a lot healthier.

Also, it's critical for you to DO the exercises we have suggested with a loving, caring, trusting partner.

Some of you might want to reinforce what you've learned from this book by watching the instructional videotape series we recently produced. If so, send us a self-addressed stamped envelope and we will send you the purchasing information (address on the back of this book).

Some of you may now wish to experience some actual self-defense training. Here are several available options:

1. You might want to take a weekend workshop with us. Send us a self-addressed stamped envelope and we will send you a schedule.

Full speed, full power
training in class

2. You could take a Model Mugging class from someone else offered locally in your area. We strongly suggest that you take a Model Mugging class only from instructors who have been certified by Matt Thomas. There have, unfortunately, been a lot of people using the Model Mugging name and armored suit but not teaching what we teach. For information about officially certified Model Mugging classes, send a self-addressed stamped envelope to the address in the back of the book.

3. If Model Mugging classes are not in your area, you may want to take another self-defense class that uses an armored assailant. There are many "copycat" programs, and although we don't recommend or endorse any of them, that does not mean you might not benefit in some way from taking one. Absorb what's useful and throw the rest away.

4. You may also be interested in studying one of the various martial arts. We recognize many values of the martial arts. I

[Matt] have studied more than twenty styles for more than thirty-two years. The most important advice we can give you with regard to any class is to watch one before you sign up. What's best for you depends more on the instructor than on the style.

But whether or not you choose to be professionally trained, we want to emphasize the importance of the mental exercises in these pages. Please don't skip them, and do revisit and repeat them from time to time. Being an evolved warrior is about mental as well as physical discipline. Continue to think about and write down appreciations, worries, and fears, turning each one into a problem with a solution, and don't forget your hopes and aspirations.

Don't just fight out of love. Live that way. Feel the power within yourself and keep on feeling it. Use that transforming power in all aspects of your life.

The Cleansing of the Storm

As you combine the physical exercises with the mental ones, let the emotions rise. Let the tears flow. Don't try to stop them. You need to release them. A Chinese proverb says, "The tears that the eyes don't weep, the organs will."

Along with the rain come the thunder and the lightning. Let the anger come up. Strike the safe surfaces, the ones that allow you to express anger without injuring yourself. Remember, when you practice heel palming:

- First three strikes—think of preserving the lives of the ones you love.

- Shake your body loose.

- Next three strikes—think of hitting those who have hurt you.

- Shake your body loose.

- Last three strikes—think of loving yourself and the things you will love doing in the future.

Combine your physical, mental, and emotional energy into the release of the anger, shouting NO with each strike.

Then let go of your anger. Bring your joy back to yourself. After the storms comes the rainbow. From the cleansing of the heavens comes the renewal of the earth.

No Ordinary Moments

Another component of being an evolved warrior is finding appreciation in all aspects of life, continually reminding yourself how precious it is and how much it is worth preserving. In this regard, we—again—find much inspiration in the words of Dan Millman, in his book *No Ordinary Moments*.

We urge our students to read it and do the exercises therein after taking our course. We suggest it to you as well.

Even if you do not follow any of this advice, try to do the following exercise every morning when you wake up:

- Lie in bed for an extra minute or two and appreciate three of your many blessings.

- Then contemplate three current worries and fears.

- Turn each worry or fear into a problem with a solution.

- Think about what you most hope for, and then figure out three ways you will aspire to accomplish that goal.

Throughout the centuries, millions of soldiers have had to go into battle, and those who have spoken and written about it describe the moments before they went off to fight as very vivid. They became intensely aware that they were alive. Their orange juice never tasted so sweet. Their lover—if they were so fortunate to have one—never felt so soft and warm.

But why, we ask, wait for battle to live life this intensely?

There are no ordinary moments.

There are no ordinary days—and our advice is to approach each day as an extraordinary event.

As you get ready for breakfast each morning, remember appreciations. Different cultures called this many things, but the most commonly known word is "grace," even for a simple cup of coffee.

When you turn on the faucet and clean, clear water—or something resembling it—pours out, appreciate that you didn't have to hike through the snow to the stream, chop a hole in the ice, and slip and slide your way back while trying to balance a bucket of water and then have to boil the water before drinking it.

Notice even your small fortunes and appreciate them.

Whatever your religious beliefs—or lack thereof—find and/or utilize some method of summarizing each day. Appreciate all of your blessings, acknowledge your fears, and transform them into problems with a solution; then consider your hopes and aspirations. If one of your fortunes is a special person in your life, be sure to share your daily appreciations and your hopes and aspirations with that person.

No Ordinary Lives

Being an evolved warrior and living life intensely can bring about remarkable change. Defending yourself, as we emphasized before, is not about hating your attackers. It's about loving yourself. When you are able to love and trust yourself in order to integrate your body, mind, and emotions to defend yourself against a threat, imagine how easily you can deal with the minor conflicts in life.

This is what makes teaching such a joy: that students—and the students of our students—come to us months or years later to thank us for the shifts and changes that have occurred in their lives.

"I've lost twenty pounds after taking your class!" is one we've heard more than once—usually by incest survivors whose extra weight can be armor to discourage anyone from being attracted to them. When they no longer required the armor—because they were no longer terrified of future attacks—they were able to lose the weight.

Not every overweight student we have ever had has lost weight after learning to defend herself (or we'd really fill our classes!), but it can happen. We once had an anorexic student have a similar success story after our class: she started eating, met a man, fell in love, got married, and had a son. She named the boy Matthew, which was an overwhelming honor, but the truth is that we had not "healed" her. She had healed herself. Model Mugging was just a turning point on her journey.

A concert pianist said that after Model Mugging, she "found passion in her music." She said that she had been afraid to become angry, and that had diluted her force as a musician. By exploring and accepting her passion in strength, she could also explore and accept her passion in tenderness.

A woman quit a job she had hated for eight years, founded her own company, and two years later was successful beyond her expectations.

A number of students found that their relationships with men improved immensely because they no longer feared them.

This has also been true for Denise:

Now that I have physical power, I can tear down the walls I had previously put up to protect myself. I can reveal the real me. I can be vulnerable and loving again. Because I no longer fear men, I can let them know who I really am. And the more I can open up, the more life can open up for me.

The majority of our students don't come back and tell us of dramatic changes in their lives, but those with whom we keep in contact almost unanimously report that the confidence they now possess, knowing they can take care of themselves, extends into all areas of their lives.

They become more assertive in their relationships with men. No, they don't respond to interpersonal conflict with a heel palm or a thigh to the groin—but they do stand up for themselves and demand mutual respect.

Having self-confidence can enable you to stand up to an abusive or condescending boss as well. If you are prepared for the garbage mouth of a rapist, you probably aren't going to be as intimidated by negative remarks from a boss. Again, you don't want to resort to a heel palm—it will probably get you fired and could get you arrested, and anyway, it isn't at all necessary—but you can hold your ground and wait for his or her storm to subside. Concentrate on your breathing! Listen! Breathe!

You can hold your ground in all kinds of circumstances. An experience Denise had not long ago is a good illustration:

I was hired to play the lead in an action movie. It was a great part and an exciting opportunity for me as an actress. There was only one problem—a topless scene in the script which I felt very uncomfortable about, in terms of my career and in terms of my own personal values. But I was concerned that I wouldn't get the movie. Before Model Mugging, I would have either gone through with the scene without a word (hating myself for doing it) or simply run away—by turning down the entire project in a moment of heated temper. Fortunately, those are no longer my only two options. With the confidence of an evolved warrior, I resolved that I would not take off my clothes, but I also resolved that I would assert myself and make my case and get the part anyway. I wrote a letter to the director—who was also the screenwriter. I began the letter with an appreciation, praising him for the gripping script he'd created and thanking him for hiring me. I then expressed my worry and fear, turning both into a problem with a solution: I had a problem with the topless scene (and told him why) and I offered some creative suggestions of ways that scene could be shot without the nudity, and ways in which my character's sexuality could be heightened without nudity. I ended the letter with the hope that he understood my point of view and still wanted me for the part—and the aspiration that if so, I would try to do the fabulous job his script deserved.

It worked.

Self-Defense Is Not a License to Harm

Beyond assertiveness, being an evolved warrior also means preserving the quality of life—not just for you and your loved ones, but, to the extent that you can, for everyone.

If confronted by any obnoxious stranger—say a rude driver or someone who cuts the line—your anger can be short-lived. Rather than stand there enraged, feeling stepped on and powerless, you should feel powerful, acknowledging to yourself that you could probably do serious bodily harm to this person, but won't because you are an evolved warrior. You have nothing to prove—to yourself or to anyone else.

Denise recently had an experience that exemplifies this:

I was on my way to the movies with some friends when I was approached by an aggressive panhandler. I guess he'd been having bad luck that evening, because when I tried to ignore him, he began yelling vulgar things at me. I was prepared to defend myself if he came any closer and, just as important, I had my psychic guard up, too, so that when he hurled his garbage mouth at me, I was unfazed. My friends could not get over the fact that the entire encounter did not bother me. Even their mentioning how it should bother me did not cause me to get upset or indignant. I honestly didn't care what he said. Once the lights in the movie theater dimmed, I forgot the whole incident and enjoyed the film.

That is power.

As you learn to defend yourself, you can live with power. By releasing your fear and letting go of your anger, you realize how much energy it took to keep these emotions suppressed. Now you have all of this energy available to you to express in creative and positive ways. Your life gets filled with joy. The more you live with this joy, the more it becomes a habit. Of course, you will go through cycles, but at least your life will become an upward spiral.

Having power allows you to be peaceful. I [Matt] have been practicing the martial arts for thirty-two years, and in my personal life I've had to hit someone on only one occasion: it was a mugger, and I had already given him my wallet and my guitar without a struggle (material possessions are not worth the use of my fists, which can easily lead to a lawsuit). But despite my cooperativeness, the guy still tried to shoot me, at which point I realized I'd better hit him. In every other personal confrontation of my adult life, I've been able to use my wits or only appropriate force to avoid conflict.

Self-Defense Is Not Therapy

Tremendous healing can take place when former rape and incest victims learn to defend themselves. Of course, we are not therapists, and so we suggest that anyone undergoing therapy use that setting in order to deal with issues brought out by the exercises in this book.

We always recommend that prospective students who are in therapy consult their therapist before taking any of our classes—

and we do so with great confidence because a number of psychologists have taken our classes and found them very beneficial as well as practical. We do not take credit for these benefits of our self-defense training. They come from within!

Self-Defense CAN Be Empowerment

At the very most, this book is a channel of empowerment, a facilitator of growth. It is up to you to make it all happen. A very splendid illustration of that is a former Model Mugging student whom we saw several years later at a reunion. The woman was visibly pregnant, and with a beaming smile she attributed her condition to Model Mugging. She had, it turned out, been pregnant once before while married to her first husband, who was abusive and beat her so severely that he killed their unborn child. This woman was now married to a decent man, but she had had great difficulty becoming pregnant—in fact, they had given up. A month after she took Model Mugging, she was pregnant. Of course, we are no more a fertility clinic than a therapy center. But she insisted that her pregnancy was no coincidence. "My body," she said, "finally knew it was safe."

This woman truly exemplified that the purpose of an evolved warrior is to preserve life. Because of her courage to become a warrior, not only did she transform her own life, she brought forth new life. Her daughter will learn from her.

And hopefully, it won't just stop there.

The final—and perhaps the paramount—responsibility of an evolved warrior is to lead by example and inspire others upward on that same path.

Person by person, our world can be transformed.

──Glossary of Movements──

Ax Kick

A very powerful kick from a side position on the ground and bringing the leg up and slamming it down at the target area. (See Chapter Five, page 88.)

Butt Strike

A backward thrusting of the hips, striking an assailant with your butt. (See Chapter Five, page 91.)

Countergrab

Grabbing the wrists of an assailant who has grabbed you by your wrists. (See Chapter Eight, page 185.)

Flanking

Maneuvering yourself against multiple assailants so that you face only one of them at a time. (See Chapter Eight, page 176.)

Freeze-Walk Stance

The defensive posture to assume whenever you feel danger. (See Chapter Four, page 54.)

Front-Thrust Kick

A less powerful—but fast and accurate—kick from a sitting position on the ground. (See Chapter Five, page 87.)

Ground Fighting

Using the reach advantage of your legs against an assailant's arms and your lower-body strength against his upper-body strength by taking the battle to ground level. (See Chapter Five, page 80.)

Hammer Fist

A closed-fist punch, underhand and backward to the assailant's groin area. (See Chapter Five, page 94.)

Heel Palm

A forward-striking punch with open hand, using the bottom of the palm as the point of impact. (See Chapter Four, page 67.)

Look and Assess

Checking your surroundings for additional dangers and testing an assailant to be sure he is unconscious and no longer poses a threat. (See Chapter Five, page 76.)

Pect-lat Lock

Flexing the pectoral and latissimus muscles by bringing the elbows together in front of the chest—which greatly increases the power of a punch. (See Chapter Four, page 57.)

Side-Thrust Kick

A very powerful kick from a side position on the ground. (See Chapter Five, page 85.)

Standing Release

A defensive maneuver to free yourself from an assailant holding you in a standing position. (See Chapter Five, page 98.)

Thigh to the Groin

A forward kick, driving the lower thigh under the assailant's groin area and then up. (See Chapter Four, page 69.)

Thigh to the Nose
  A forward kick (usually following a thigh to the groin) using the lower thigh and driving it upward into the assailant's head. (See Chapter Four, page 71.)

MATT THOMAS is a world class martial artist with multiple black belts in Judo, Karate, Kendo, and the Russian art of SOMBO, who has made a life's work of teaching the program of self-defense described in this book. He founded the first Model Mugging program over twenty-four years ago. Matt has trained thousands of law enforcement, SWAT, and hostage rescue teams as an unarmed and armed defensive tactics instructor. Matt earned both his BS and MA in Biology from Stanford University. He is the coauthor, with Bob Bishop, of *Protecting Children from Danger*.

DENISE LOVEDAY is Matt's co-instructor in the Model Mugging course, an accomplished actress, and producer of television and film projects. She graduated from the College of Communications at the University of Texas in Austin, where she specialized in film production.

LARRY STRAUSS has authored and coauthored many nonfiction books, including *When You Have Chest Pain, Diets That Work,* and *The Magic Man*. He recently published his first novel, *Fake Out*.

MARIO PRADO is a professional photographer who has shot illustrations for ten martial arts texts and covers for martial arts magazines including *Blackbelt*.

Matt, Denise and other teams of instructors have taught Model Mugging, an innovative and highly effective method of self-defense to over 30,000 women, children and men around the country. Together they create a loving and supportive environment where victims of attacks can heal the aftershocks of assault; it offers all students a new sense of empowerment in their personal lives.

For more information contact:
Matt Thomas, Model Mugging
859 North Hollywood Way, #127
Burbank, California 91505
(818) 843-1848